So You Graduated College...

A Financial Guide to Life After Graduation

Published by Keystone Enterprises LLC
Los Altos, CA

Cover Design by Budget Book Design, New York, NY
Printed by RJ Communications, New York, NY

ISBN #: 0-9785149-0-4

Disclaimer

Best efforts were made by the author of *So You Graduated College* and Keystone Enterprises, LLC to provide factual and useful information for the recent college graduate. This publication was designed to be used as a general financial guide. Neither the publisher nor the author is in the business of rendering legal, financial, or other professional advice and if legal or expert assistance is required, the services of a professional should be sought. The author and publisher disclaim any and all liability that is incurred, directly or indirectly, from the use or application of the contents of this book.

Purchasing Information

Check out our website at www.soyougraduatedcollege.com for ordering information. Significant discounts are offered on bulk orders and book customization options, such as including a congratulatory letter, are also available.

Table of Contents

Note to Reader

You graduated! Woo-hoooooo! No more school! Call the relatives, throw your backpack out the window, and pop open the champagne! This is a great accomplishment and you should be proud. But beware, real life is lurking nearby, and as the celebration surrounding graduation fades away, it will come at you like a bat out of hell. Rent, insurance, food, car payments—you will have to pay for them all. This fact is not meant to scare you, but rather to entice you to learn about the financial world—not in the theoretical way taught in textbooks, but rather in a more practical sense that is applicable to real life.

So how should you acquire such knowledge? By reading this book, of course. But before you begin, I have one small request. While reading this book, take into consideration everything that is said, but do not believe any of it until you have first questioned it. Like many books, this book is simply one person's perspective on life. Some of the information may be invaluable, but some may be completely useless to you. It is up to you to decipher amongst it all to determine what is applicable to your specific situation. Continuously question if what makes sense for me will make sense for you. The point of this book is not to tell you how to live your life or how to handle your finances. Instead, its purpose is to simply share my perspective and to help you make informed financial decisions in the future. When it comes to finances, too many people simply walk a random path or, even worse, blindly join the herd following the advice of others. Don't leave your financial future in the hands of chance. Know yourself—your needs, your desires, your fears—and know the world around you. Doing so will guide you down a prosperous and, if you choose, wealthy path.

Chapter 1

CAREER & GRAD SCHOOL

What's Next?

So you graduated college. Congratulations! But what now? Up until graduation, your entire life was probably planned for you: elementary school, junior high, high school, and then college. None of it was an option—you simply followed the path laid before you. But now this path has come to an end, and you are confronted with an infinite number of possibilities and nobody to direct you in the "right" direction. So what do you do? Get a master's degree? Start your career? Travel the world? Go to law school? Party every night till the sun comes up?

The choice is yours. Although the time period following graduation can be full of uncertainty and concern, it is also very exciting. The world is at your fingertips— you can do anything you want. The important thing is that you do what you want and not what others expect of you. If your college and post-college experience is anything like mine, then I'm sure that answering the question, "So what are you going to do with your life?" is becoming very tiresome. Everyone recognizes how big a transition the post-college period is and are therefore extremely interested in which path you choose to embark upon. Although such interest in your life should be appreciated, the problem is that, hidden within that interest, there is pressure on you to take one particular path. As a generalization, it definitely seems that society is prone to pressure recent grads towards career advancement. You may share those same ambitions and so may view the pressure as encouragement, which is great. However, if you value a transitional period in which you can contemplate life, then you may find the pressure unwelcome.

Wherever your desires lay, make sure to follow them and not the desires of others. I can't emphasize enough the benefits that come from enjoying your career and life path. In the book The Millionaire Mind, Thomas J. Stanley examines thousands of self-made millionaires and explains what makes them tick. One of the most prevalent characteristics of America's most wealthy individuals is a love for their career. This should not come as a surprise. Having passion makes success all the more probable. But, more importantly, enjoying what you do allows you to wake up every morning with a smile. Can you imagine being miserable at work every day? Unfortunately, this is reality for too many Americans. So do what you love and the money will follow—well, maybe not always, but do what you hate and the money will definitely not follow.

The Salary Obsession

One problematic issue that is widespread among recent graduates is the obsession with salary. A high salary is great, but regardless, I urge you to temporarily ignore the paycheck and instead consider the experiences and knowledge potential each job has to offer. At this stage in life, your lifestyle is probably less expensive than it will ever be again and because you have so many years ahead of you, the potential benefits of knowledge and experience are greater now than they will ever be. As Robert Kiyosaki says in his book, Rich Dad Poor Dad, "Keep using your brain, work for free, and soon your mind will show you ways of making money far beyond what I could ever pay you." Well, you probably don't always want to work for free – we all have at least some bills to pay, but regardless, he makes a good point. Everyone loves a high salary, but don't merely chase the higher salaries as there are many more important considerations in making a career choice. Instead, chase the knowledge, experience, and other door-opening opportunities because, in the long run, this path will prove to be much more profitable—not only for your wallet, but also for your mind and soul. Think about some of the options you have right now or even those you had when you were in college.

For example, while I was attending college, I could have worked construction and made around $20/hour. Most students in a college town earn minimum wage, so $20/hour would have been terrific. But think about what else the construction job had to offer. For someone planning on entering construction management or a related field, it might have been a great choice, but those were not my plans. I would have been working purely for a paycheck. Instead, I pursued a job in a real estate investment office as well as a job as a teaching assistant for the finance professor at my college. Both of these jobs paid about half of what the construction job would have, but were certainly worth my time, because through them I was not only presented with many favorable employment opportunities upon graduation, but I also learned a great deal about the financial world and gained invaluable insight. Most other college jobs could not have provided such things. So don't worry about the money for now, as tempting as it can be. If you can just focus on developing your career, and more importantly, developing yourself, then the money will eventually be thrown at you in much greater quantities.

Invest in Yourself

Perhaps the most valuable asset you have is your brain. Just as you would invest in and maintain a physical asset such as a house by remodeling and performing regular maintenance, consider investing in and maintaining your mind. Read books, take classes through the local college, teach yourself a new skill, or sign up for a master's program. Such self-investment will prove to be highly beneficial in the long run regardless of your career choice. Unlike money invested in the stock market, knowledge and skills cannot be easily lost, which makes them much more powerful assets. Life can throw you many curve balls. The more you expand your skill set, the more home runs you will hit.

The number one rule of investing in financial assets is to diversify, diversify, and diversify. The same rule applies to self-investment. Society does tend to monetarily reward those who develop a single skill or subject and make it their life's work. However, just as an investor who invests only in the stock market is highly vulnerable to market crashes, a person who only dedicates him or herself only to a single subject is highly vulnerable to life's curve balls. You never know what might happen in the future so it would be in your best interest to have other skills to fall back on in case you suddenly find yourself unable to continue working in your current field. You may sustain an injury or other health complication that prevents you from being successful in certain careers or you may have the almost inevitable revelation that you don't want to do the same damn thing your entire life. The more options you can create for yourself, the safer your future financial and mental well being.

On the flip side, you don't necessarily want to spread yourself too thin. Like most parts of life, you need to find a balance. There is too much knowledge and too many skills in this world for our brains to handle, so we must be selective. The natural choice is to go with what you enjoy. It is extremely difficult to excel in something you dislike, so you might as well focus on learning skills that not only develop your brain and resume, but leave you smiling at the end of the day. And don't just limit yourself to resume-building skills. The power of knowledge is undeniable whether it's in regards to career, vacation, or everyday life. Take a CPR class and you may save someone's life. Learn about automobiles and you can prevent a mechanic from ripping you off. Read a book on adding spice to your relationship and your lover will be amazed by your ability to...well, just imagine that one.

Getting on Your Boss's Good Side

In the work world, the most worthy candidate always gets the job, promotion, or raise. Right? Wrong! That would be nice, but in reality, the hiring, firing, and promoting processes are carried out by subjective, biased people just like you and me. Similar to the revelation we all seem to have after the first few years of college that our parents don't have the answers to everything, after a short time in the work world you will discover that your boss does not always make the right decision either. If you desire a promotion, raise, or letter of recommendation, you want to make sure that your boss's actions, whether good or bad, right or wrong, are in your best interest. Here are a few tips to make sure you are on your boss's good side:

Avoid Emotions at Work

Generally speaking, emotions are not welcome at work – at least not negative emotions. Every boss wants to work with "professionals." Although the definition of professionalism certainly varies from person to person and job to job, nobody includes whining or yelling in that definition. Much of a person's life is spent at work, which can be an emotional environment. However, there is a time and place for everything and negative emotions are just not welcome at work. On the other hand, you don't necessarily want to hold all feelings inside, as we all know that can be unhealthy. If something at work is really bothering you, let it be known, but let it be known in a professional manner. Don't whine or yell and choose the right time to bring up the issue. Don't get caught in the heat of the moment and don't interrupt your boss during a meeting just to complain. Think about why you are upset and, if you believe your emotions to be valid, calmly explain your problem to the appropriate person and suggest a fair solution. It is important to choose your battles though. You do not want to appear to be a habitual complainer.

Avoid Gossip in the Workplace

There is almost nothing constructive or positive about gossip. Although it may be fun at the moment, it will more than likely come back to bite you in the butt. If you engage in gossip with another coworker, don't expect the conversation to remain confidential. If that person is spilling secrets to you, then he or she will probably do the same with others. The quickest way to get on someone's bad side is to gossip about the person. Higher-level employees look down on such pastimes and by participating, you are placing yourself in a risky position when it comes to issues such as promotions, lay offs, raises, and vacation time. Yes, gossip can be quite entertaining, but try to resist while at work. You don't want to say anything that could possibly be used against you in the future. Don't think that you can't have fun at work though—just don't gossip.

Know Who to Impress

Not everyone in the workplace is worthy of your best behavior. Know who holds the power at work and whose opinion the boss respects. Then focus your energy towards impressing them.

Personality Can Go a Long Way

In reality, the most qualified employee does not always receive the most rewards. In many cases, it is the most liked employee who is rewarded. Don't be afraid to express yourself at work and especially at work parties, feel free to let loose. I'm definitely not saying to get drunk and pass out on your boss's lawn, but everyone likes a person who knows how to have a good time. Take a social risk and tell a funny story or crack a joke (stay away from sexual and racial jokes though). Try to be friendly, outgoing, and polite—especially with your boss—and you never know what doors may open.

If You Went the Extra Mile, Let It Be Known
Modesty is often appreciated in our personal lives, but it does not always get rewarded in the work world. This is not because your boss does not like modesty but because the workplace is often hectic, and unless pointed out, extra efforts can go unnoticed. The boss can't reward accomplishments that she did not know existed. Don't be cocky with your success, but do let your efforts be noticed.

Tit for Tat
If you ask for something, offer something in return. For example, if you want to leave work early one day, offer to work overtime another day. Or if you don't want a certain assignment, offer to take on another assignment instead (perhaps a more challenging and more exciting assignment). Just make sure that your boss feels like he is receiving something in return for whatever favor he is granting. This way it feels like more of a deal than a demand.

Don't Be Lazy
I know how great it can feel to have nothing going on at work and be able to search the Internet all day, send emails to friends, practice juggling erasers, or whatever it is you enjoy doing on your downtime. During downtime at my first job, whenever a coworker would walk by my cubicle, I would click over on my computer from Internet to some random Excel spreadsheet that I pretended to be working on. Although everyone thought I was working, I wasn't really scoring any points with anyone. Eventually, when I felt like I had reached the end of the Internet, I began asking the head honcho if I could take on extra assignments. I can't tell you how much that is appreciated in the workplace. Supervisors and managers often feel overwhelmed and they really value an employee who is willing to lend a hand above and beyond what is requested.

Balancing Your Life

You often hear people preaching about the importance of finding a niche. By becoming the most knowledgeable person about something specific, say ... the bizarre mating rituals of the pacific octopus, you will likely be monetarily rewarded. The world is always in need of experts (yes, even octopus sex experts) and is willing to pay considerable amounts of money for their knowledge and advice. Expert witnesses in a court case, for example, often have an hourly wage between $100/hour and $250/hour. These people are not lawyers, they are simply experts in their field. My uncle, for example, is the #1 guy in California on termite damage and he charges $200/hour for his time.

So finding a niche and becoming an expert can be quite lucrative. However, consider the costs. In order to become the best of the best, you will need to make considerable sacrifices. All of your energy needs to be focused on advancing your career or expertise, which leaves you with little time for other activities. This means less time with friends and family, less time for your investments, and less time for hobbies. Your professional life may reward this level of expertise, but a gratifying personal life requires greater diversity. It's often more satisfying on a personal level to be an average employee, an average investor, an average husband, and an average father rather than a horrible investor, a horrible husband, and a horrible father, yet a highly paid professional. At least that's my two cents.

Self-Employment

Self-employment is not typical for a recent graduate. In fact, it's not all that typical for the older crowd either. However, with ambition and a little discipline, self-employment is definitely attainable.

Pros of Self-Employment:

> *You are Your Own Boss.* You and you alone determine what you do each day. If you want to spend the day snowboarding instead of working, that's your call. If you have a hangover from a crazy Tuesday night, sleep in—again, it's your call.

➢ *The Tax Deductions.* When you own your own business, your income is determined by subtracting your business expenses from your earnings. What are considered expenses though? Your opinion is as good as mine. There is a lot of gray area here. For example, if you use a computer in your business, you can deduct the purchase of a laptop. Meals, travel, client entertainment, and many other expenses can all be deducted as well. So if you take a client to a football game ... sounds like a deduction to me. Just call it client appreciation expenditures and it's fair game. Use your imagination. There is a lot of opportunity for these sorts of deductions—just make sure they are legit and defensible.

➢ *Higher Earnings.* Well, at least in theory. As an employee, the work you perform has benefits to the company. If converted to a dollar amount, the benefits you provide should be greater than your salary. The difference is the company's profit. If the company was not earning money from your employment, they would probably fire you. As a self-employed person, you are your own employee and your own boss, so in theory you should have more income.

➢ *Retirement Savings.* A self-employed individual is generally allowed to contribute much more to her retirement accounts than an employee. As you will discover in Chapter 11, the benefits of tax deferral in retirement accounts can be extraordinary.

Cons of Self-employment:

➢ *It's Risky.* When you are self-employed, nothing is guaranteed. In January, your paycheck might be huge, but in February it may be non-existent. Even worse, your business could fail and all that time, energy, and money would go down the drain. It is generally a risky endeavor, but taking on such risk is often rewarded.

➢ *Benefits, What Benefits?* A person who is self-employed has no benefits and has to set up his or her own insurance and retirement plans.

> *Hard Work.* Almost everybody who has started a successful business of some kind or another will agree that it is a lot of hard work. A self-employed person is not only the owner of his or her own company, but also the manager, the secretary, and the accountant. Particularly in the beginning, when you are still learning the ropes, there may be a lot of late nights and weekends dedicated to your business.

> *Liability.* If you get sued for your actions as an employee, then you are generally not liable because you were acting as an agent on your company's behalf. A self-employed person, though, IS the company and is therefore exposed to the risk of lawsuits. However...

Limited Liability Companies

Anyone who is self-employed in some form or another may want to consider starting an LLC, or Limited Liability Company. As its name implies, an LLC provides you with limited liability. Without an LLC, you are vulnerable to being sued for all of your business assets as well as all of your personal assets. Under an LLC, only your business assets are at risk. The LLC is considered a separate entity. When profits are earned, they are distributed to you and any other partners. You can basically consider yourself as an employee of the LLC. If you're an employee and your company gets sued, can the lawyers take away your house or car? Of course not! You're just an employee. The lawyers can take only assets of the business. The same is true for an LLC. Once the LLC (you) cuts the employee (also you) a check, then that money is safe. As a self-employed individual, it is one of the best kinds of insurance you can get.

I recently started an LLC in California and had to pay $70 to file the application and $800 each year as an annual tax. These expenses can be deducted on your taxes though, which will somewhat mitigate the impact on your wallet. All you really have to do is pay the fees and fill out a form and you have formed an LLC. A few states require at least two members, but most require only one person.

If you are self-employed, have a side business, or are in a partnership, at least consider forming an LLC. The benefits are great and the limitations few. Check with your specific state's business department for fees and limitations, as they tend to vary.

Graduate School?

There may not be a better way to advance your career than going to grad school. These days, a bachelor's degree is nothing—everyone has one. I think you can buy one on eBay for two dollars now! In order to succeed, you need a differential—something to set yourself apart from all the other graduates. This differential can be achieved through internships, exceptional academic performance, good connections, or prior work experience, but perhaps the best way to take your resume to the next level is by going to graduate school. In fact, in the business world, employees without an M.B.A. tend to hit a ceiling on the promotional ladder and watch their M.B.A.-holding coworkers climb right past them. Unfortunately, society doesn't always recognize a person's true level of competence or potential. Instead, some standard way of measuring that competence is needed, which often comes in the form of a graduate degree. A graduate degree should provide you with invaluable knowledge and a memorable experience, but at the least, it will instill confidence in others that you know your stuff.

Of course, there is also a downside to graduate school: it is costly and time consuming. In fact, studies have shown a negative correlation between graduate school and wealth. If you think about it, this makes sense. For example, a person with a Ph.D. may have dedicated five years to pursuing an education while earning no money and paying tuition. Meanwhile, all her peers are earning money and accumulating savings. Although the Ph.D. student will likely become a more marketable employee with a higher future salary, she sacrificed five years of income and investment potential.

Regardless of your career path, there is almost guaranteed to be some kind of master's degree, certificate program, or professional school out there for you. Just make sure to weigh the costs and benefits of the program and make sure that it is what you want – not what your parents, your peers, or society in general desires for you.

Check with the career center at your college, or any nearby college, to see if there will be any information sessions on the particular graduate program that you are interested in. Most colleges offer informational lectures and Q&A sessions on popular graduate programs. These can be great resources for planning your future. Also, each year U.S. News publishes a magazine called Exclusive Rankings of America's Best Graduate Schools, which can be very useful when deciding where to apply.

How to Pay for Grad School

Grad school can be extremely expensive. Tuition alone is often around $25,000 per year for a good law, business, or medical school. Luckily there are ways to minimize, and sometimes even eliminate, those costs.

Traditional Financial Aid

Financial aid is readily available for most graduate programs. Apply for as much as you can find. Scholarships and fellowships are preferable to loans for the obvious reason that the money does not need to be paid back. Some financial aid is rewarded purely on a needs basis, giving preferential treatment to those who need it the most, but there are also many scholarships and grants that are awarded on a merit basis—and these are not limited to academic achievement. Scholarships and grants can be awarded for many other reasons, such as athletic ability, community service, or any combination of unique criteria that you just might meet. Check with the school for available aid and also check the Internet. Two great starting points are www.finaid.org and www.fastweb.com.

Student Loans

Perhaps the most common method of financing graduate school is with student loans. Interest rates on these loans are usually relatively low, at least when compared to consumer debt, and payments typically do not begin until six months after graduation. There are two general types: subsidized and unsubsidized. Subsidized loans are much more preferable because interest is not charged until repayment begins. With an unsubsidized loan, interest is charged starting the day the loan is originated. You don't have to pay the interest until repayment begins, but it is tacked on to the amount you owe. For example, if you borrow $50,000 through an unsubsidized loan, after you graduate you may owe around $60,000. If the loan was subsidized, you would still owe only $50,000.

If upon graduation you can prove that you have "special circumstances," such as the inability to land a job or some other economic hardship, then you may be granted an extension of up to three years to begin repayment of your loan.

Generally speaking, consumer debt is evil, but borrowing money for an investment can be very beneficial. In this case, you are investing in your education. The skills and knowledge you are acquiring will likely result in significant social and financial benefits, thereby justifying the debt.

The Parents
Another great place to check for scholarships is with the folks. Ask your parents how they feel about helping you out with graduate school. Depending on their financial situation, they may at least be willing to help with a portion of it.

Your Employer
Even better than your parents is your employer. Many employers are willing to fund a graduate program as long as it is relative to your job. This is particularly common with M.B.A. programs in the business world and also for the less intense certificate programs offered at many university extensions. But for law or medical school, you're probably on your own. If your employer is willing to pay for grad school, it's hard to pass up. Sure you'll have to dedicate some time and effort, but getting an M.B.A. or other degree for free is a great deal. There is one small catch though—you often have to commit to working for that company for a specified time period. Check with your employer to see what the company's requirements are.

529 Plans
If you are planning on working upon graduation and then going back to school sometime in the future, you may want to consider using a Qualified Tuition Plan (also called a 529 plan) or a Coverdell ESA. Under these plans, your money is allowed to grow tax free as long as it is used for educational

purposes. Similar to the Individual Retirement Account example on page 124, this tax-free growth can be quite beneficial. If the money is not used for educational expenses, not only is tax due on the withdrawals, but a 10% penalty is also charged. If you have not used this money by the age of 30, then you will be subject to taxes and the 10% penalty. However, you can avoid this tax and penalty if you roll the account over to a younger family member.

Working While Attending Grad School

One of the best employment opportunities available for graduate students is right there on campus. Research and teaching assistant positions are often reserved for graduate students and, in my experience, provide an extremely high salary relative to the level of effort involved. If you're lucky enough to work with a friendly and knowledgeable faculty member, you might just learn something too.

Other Considerations

You are allowed to make penalty-free withdrawals from an Individual Retirement Account as long as the money is used for higher education. Also, make sure to minimize your tax bill by deducting qualified higher education expenses up to the limit and by taking advantage of the HOPE and Lifetime Learning tax credits on your federal tax form.

Chapter 1: What It's All About

Attending graduate school and starting a career are huge choices and should not be taken lightly. Make sure you are not overly persuaded by the opinions of others and are true to yourself. Following your desires is the key to success.

Chapter **2**

FRUGAL LIVING

Living within Your Means

Perhaps the best way to accumulate great wealth is to not throw it away upon arrival. Sounds like common sense, right? Well, it is, but much of the world does not follow this simple advice. Because of strong influences such as the media, our peers, and even our own burning desires, the drive to consume and "live the good life" is widespread amongst the college and freshly graduated crowd. There are definitely benefits to living beyond your means—after all, who wouldn't want to hop in their Beamer, cruise down to Las Vegas to stay at the MGM Grand, have a few drinks, see a few shows, and go clubbing. Unfortunately there are future costs to this kind of lifestyle, which in my opinion, far outweigh the temporary gratification provided. You can still live an exciting and fun life, but why a beamer and why the MGM Grand? What's wrong with driving a Honda Civic, staying at the Flamingo, eating at the $9.99 buffets, and taking advantage of the only guaranteed win in Vegas (the free drinks!)?

The bitter truth is that you can live beyond your means only temporarily. Eventually, you will be forced to live below your means in order to pay off the past. The resulting problem is not only a financial issue, but a psychological one as well. An increase in quality of life is welcomed, yet a decrease is feared. If you spoil yourself as a young adult with a high standard of living, you are setting yourself up for disappointment in the future when your standard of living will likely decrease or at least stay the same.

Think about these unrealistic yet meaningful examples to better illustrate my point. Whose life would be happier as a whole: a girl who was born a princess but lost her crown and became poor or a poor girl who became a princess? How would you feel if you had to trade in your cell phone for a pager? I was happy when I had a pager, and happy again when I got a cell phone, but I would be upset if I had to go back to having a pager. The point is simply that you're better off starting at the bottom of a hill and climbing up than starting at the top and rolling down. You will likely be happier living below your means now and then steadily and happily increasing your quality of life as you age.

It may be difficult to force yourself to live within your means when you have the ability to live beyond them. However, assuming you like to have things and do things that cost money, I encourage you to wait. Hold off on the luxuries in life because if you wait you will be able to experience them in much greater quantities. For example, if you bought an old Toyota Corolla instead of that brand new SUV, and placed the difference in a stock market account, you could buy six SUVs in 20 years when the investment matures. Or you could go on 30 trips to Hawaii in 40 years when you retire instead of one now. This isn't to say that you should not spend money now and have fun. You just need to be aware of the tradeoffs involved. Extravagant spending when you are young places a choke hold on your finances and will delay, if not prevent, the accomplishment of many future goals.

The Truth About Millionaires

When many people hear the term "millionaire," they automatically think about celebrities like P-Diddy bling-blingin in their fancy sports cars and huge mansions. The truth, however, is far from this fantasy. A relatively small percentage of millionaires actually own the sort of things that we have come to associate them with. Shockingly, P-Diddy is not the typical millionaire. According to the book The Millionaire Next Door, a statistical analysis of millionaires in America by Thomas J. Stanley, most millionaires wear inexpensive clothes and drive average cars yet spend heavily on financial services and education. The book goes into a detailed analysis of the millionaire lifestyle, which more often than not, is far from the stereotypical celebrity life America has grown to lust over.

It is often confusing to people why millionaires don't indulge in luxuries. After all, they can easily afford to do so. However, the reason they have such wealth is because they have avoided such luxuries. It's just plain common sense—how can someone expect to be rich if he or she constantly spends everything that is earned? You don't see many millionaires spending excessively because, if they did, they would quickly lose their millionaire status. They are frugal. It is in their nature and contributes to their success. Bottom line—you can't have your cake and eat it too. Ignoring this obvious lesson will result in many financial problems. Look at M.C. Hammer. He lived the excessively luxurious hip-hop lifestyle before anyone and last I checked, he was claiming bankruptcy and trading food stamps for baggy pants. As my old finance professor used to say, "You have two choices when it comes to money: you can look affluent or you can be affluent." Hammer chose to look affluent.

Expensive Daily Habits

Most people don't think twice about spending a few bucks here and there on the everyday things of life. When people try to cut down on their expenses, they usually focus on the larger expenses, such as rent, car payments, utility bills, etc. However, in time, that Starbucks cappuccino each day can put a significant dent in your bank account. For example, let's say that instead of buying lunch each day at work for $6, you brown-bag it for an estimated $2.50. Assuming you invested the difference in the stock market, with an estimated 10% annual return, you would have $14,400 after 10 years. Or $1.2 million in 50 years! Step back and take a look at your life. I'm sure that most of us can find a number of small daily expenses that we can somehow avoid. I'm not saying to be the cheapest person alive. I'm simply saying that it is important to recognize and understand the fact that life is full of tradeoffs. If a cup of coffee every day is worth giving up a nice car or vacation in the future, by all means buy the coffee. Just realize what you are giving up and understand the tradeoffs involved. Ask yourself what your priorities are in life and allow those priorities to guide your daily habits.

Going Out to Eat

Going out to eat can be a very expensive habit. It does have many social benefits when others are included, and I would never recommend bailing on a friend's birthday dinner to save a few bucks. However, eating everyday meals, such as lunch on a workday, at restaurants can add up quite quickly. A decent meal can easily be made at home for under $3 and if you go that route each day at work instead of getting a Subway sandwich meal for $7, you will save $1,000 over the course of a year. Going out to dinner often costs twice the amount of a Subway lunch and if you make that a regular habit, imagine how quickly your savings will dwindle. Food may be a necessity, but large expenditures on food are not. It's easy to downplay the importance of saving $4. But consider the $1,000 it will add up to each year. Now, that is something to get excited for and you can have it by simply making a small change in your eating habits.

Saving Money at the Grocery Store

Rent or mortgage payments aside, food is perhaps the largest expense that recent graduates face, so it is important that you learn how to shop. There are a number of ways to save money on groceries, but do keep in mind the importance of health. Don't starve yourself or survive on Top Ramen just because it is cheaper. The easiest method to save cash on groceries is to simply buy cheaper versions of the same product. Name brand products almost always cost more than generic brands, which leads us to the question we should always ask ourselves when price differences exist: Is the difference justified? Consider vitamins, for example. High-performance brands may provide 2,000% of the daily value of certain vitamins and/or minerals, but your body needs only 100% and studies have shown that the generic brand is almost always sufficient.

Before you knock it, try it. Buy the generic brand for your next food purchase. If you truly are unhappy with it, no big deal; it's only a few bucks, don't buy it next time. However, if you are happy with the generic brand, then you can save a lot of cash over the long haul. Consumers often mislead themselves into believing that a more expensive name brand equates to higher quality. In actuality, most of the extra cost goes towards the name, not improved quality. It costs a lot of money to have the hottest new celebrity diva shaking her butt in a television commercial while drinking a Pepsi. Some manufacturers will even produce a single product and then sell it in two different packages—one a generic non-marketed brand and the other a heavily marketed name brand. It is essentially the same product, but by selling two different packages the company can capture more of the consumer surplus (yeah, you nerdy econ majors out there know what I'm talking about). The company can sell their product at a low price to the people who will not pay more for brand names and then also sell it at a higher price to those who are willing to pay. Personally, I prefer to buy the same product at the lower price. The following are some other ideas to help save money on groceries:

> ➢ If you are shopping for more than one person or you are a big eater, go to a wholesale food retailer such as Costco or Sam's Club. You will have to buy in bulk, but the deals are often

unbeatable. (A two-foot-tall, five-pound bag of tortilla chips for $4—you can't beat that!)

➢ Keep your eyes open for good deals. I personally don't think coupons are worth collecting. They seem to be more of a hassle than they are worth. However, do take advantage of the sales and the "buy one, get one free" deals. Instead of using a shopping list, consider planning your meals around what is a good deal at the grocery store and postpone buying other items until they are on sale.

➢ When something you really like is on sale, stock up on it— as long as it is non-perishable. You're going to buy it again anyway, so you might as well buy a lot now when it is on sale. I currently have eight boxes of my favorite cereal in my pantry because they were two for the price of one.

➢ Try to avoid shopping on an empty stomach. When people are craving food, they tend to buy more than they really need. Not only will you likely come home with more groceries than you need (which of course is a waste of money), but you are also more likely to buy unhealthy food.

The Brand Name Game

Here's a fun way to discover if you're a name brand snob or if you really prefer the "higher quality." Get together with some friends and have a taste test. I've always done it with beer, which is probably why I found it enjoyable, but I guess the concept works with any food or drink that has several brand options. Designate one friend as the server and have him serve one kind of beer at a time in a small cup and not let anyone know what brand it is. Write down on a piece of paper whether you like it or not and take a guess at the brand. Go on to additional rounds with a different beer each time. After everyone has tasted all the different beers, it's time to choose your favorite and least favorite. This is the moment of truth where the classy guy who refuses to drink anything but Heineken finds out that his favorite beer is Pabst Blue Ribbon. If you discover that you like cheaper beer, wine, frozen pizza, or whatever it is that you are tasting, then why continue to buy the more expensive brand? It's often an image thing, and I know everyone wants to look cool. Remember though, you have two choices in life: you can look affluent or you can be affluent.

Saturday Night at the Bars

For those of you who enjoy going downtown to the bars on Friday and Saturday nights, be careful. Alcohol is quite skilled at stealing your money. Not only do bars charge five times the price that grocery stores charge, but on top of that you are expected to tip the bartender for simply cracking open your beer. What's up with that? Here are some ways to minimize your bar tab:

> ➢ Don't use your credit card or at least don't leave a tab open. Cocktail waitresses and bartenders are only human and on busy nights errors are not uncommon. If you pay cash, you know you paid the right amount. Also, only using cash can limit your power to make the drunken decision to buy everyone a round of beers.

> ➢ Alright girls, I'm picking on you with this one. Drop the cosmopolitans and strawberry daiquiris and split a pitcher of Bud Light with your buddies. Mixed drinks may taste good, but they're a rip-off.

> ➢ Always go with the cheap beer. If you're worried about looking cheap, you shouldn't—it's just a beer, but if you are worried, get it draft and nobody will even notice.

> ➢ If you're with a group of people, split a pitcher. It's always a better deal.

> ➢ By the way, if you're the designated driver, many bars will give you free non-alcoholic drinks.

> ➢ Most importantly, make sure to save some cash for the cab ride home because you gotta admit, drinking and driving is one of the dumbest damn things you can do. It always cracks me up when I hear the line "I've had five beers and you only had three, so you drive." In my opinion, it doesn't matter if

I've had two or ten. Either way, if I get pulled over, it's a DUI and I lose my license for a long time. Just take a cab and pick up your car the next day.

What Does it Mean to be "Cheap"?

I want to share some insight on the true meaning of the word "cheap." The term may be used throughout this book, but I don't really believe in the word's implications. There's no such thing as cheap. Instead, people simply have different priorities—that's all it is. The other night I was called cheap by a friend for searching a restaurant menu for the least expensive meal. It's not that I am cheap, it's just that expensive meals are not a priority for me. I would rather spend my money on other things such as the $700 wakeboard and the $500 guitar that I purchased earlier this month. I had no problem making these purchases because they are priorities for me. Claiming somebody is cheap is a totally subjective statement. All it really means is that the person's opinion regarding money's intended purpose differs from your own. Another common conflict people have is that of valuing free time. Many "cheap" individuals simply place greater value on their free time. If they were frivolous spenders, they would have to give up free time in order to work longer hours so that they could finance their expensive lifestyles. So don't be insulted if somebody calls you cheap. Just smile and realize that all they are saying is that your priorities differ from their own, and there is nothing wrong with that.

Dating

First off, when it comes to relationship and love issues, I encourage you not to approach them with a logical or financial mindset, as it will likely get you into trouble. But that's not what this book is about, so that being said, keep in mind that there are plenty of ways to have a good time with that special someone while hanging on to your money. Unless you want to look like a cheapskate though, you will need to substitute a little creativity for your wallet. There are many free or inexpensive things in life—you just have to use your head. I'm not saying you should take your date to Taco Bell for chalupas. I'm just saying that there is a lot of truth to the cliché "It's the thought that counts." It's not the money that counts, it's the thought, but if you have neither, you're screwed. So if you choose to go cheap, just make sure to go big and cheap. The possibilities are endless, but here are a few inexpensive yet thoughtful ideas that have worked out well for me in the past. I hope they spark some creative ideas of your own.

> ➤ I wrote and sang a song on the guitar to my girlfriend. (Even if it's awful, they'll still love it).

> ➤ I took a blanket, some snacks, and a bottle of wine and hung out with my girlfriend on a hill overlooking the San Francisco Bay Area at night. Could there be a better recipe for a little hanky-panky?

> ➤ Instead of buying a bouquet of flowers, I often made my own by driving around the neighborhood and gathering flowers. In my opinion, the bouquets were better than the ones in the store. If done well, your girlfriend will probably just assume you bought the flowers.

> ➤ I downloaded a number of karaoke love songs and recorded my own CD as a Valentine's Day present to my girlfriend. It sounded terrible, but she loved it.

> ➤ I separated the front and back seats of my car with a curtain and had my friend (disguised as a limo driver) take my girlfriend and me to dinner. I lined the ceiling with limo lights (A.K.A. Christmas lights) and had an ice chest full of champagne in the back.

> ➤ Back in high school, I had my senior prom dinner in a U-haul truck. Sounds trashy, I know, but hold on. A few friends and I rented the biggest truck available and put in picnic tables covered with tablecloths. We went all out with decorative blankets to cover the aluminum walls, Christmas lights, a goldfish bowl, candles, a TV and VCR, a CD player, a sofa bed, and a cooler full of champagne. Our dates were shocked when we took them to a U-haul truck in a parking lot for dinner, but they all loved it and will never forget that prom dinner. Unfortunately, my girlfriend went home early and I ended up passing out on the sofa bed next to my buddy Joe. Oh, well.

Take what you will from these examples. You may view them as great ideas or you may see them as ridiculous attempts to impress a significant other. Regardless, my point is simple: the most memorable dates are often the most creative. Luckily, last time I checked, money is not a requirement for creativity.

Clothing

When it comes to clothing, don't give in to all the widespread societal pressures. Just go everywhere in your birthday suit. Let it all hang out. Clothes are expensive, and by always being butt-naked, your savings will grow astronomically. It just makes sense.

I'm only kidding, of course. Clothing is such a personal thing that I cannot really give advice. There are of course lots of good deals at thrift shops, discount stores, outlets, etc., but style and trends are often such important factors with our generation that these stores often just don't cut it. As cool as Goodwill is, I guess it's no Abercrombie. If having a cool pair of shoes or sexy designer jeans makes you happy, then it is money well spent. Who am I or anyone else to tell you what you should wear or what should provide you with happiness? Just be aware of how expensive trendy clothing can be and make sure it's worth it. But girls, do you really need 20 damn pairs of shoes? And 15 pairs of sandals? I know, I know—they're cute and go with different outfits.

Traveling

When it comes to traveling, the recent grad is faced with a dilemma. Having no children and having an endless supply of energy makes your age the best time to travel, but now is also the point in your life where you probably have the least amount of money. But if traveling is in your blood, then get our there and enjoy the world. This may contradict many of the frugality guidelines previously discussed, but the perspective on life that you will gain and the experiences you will enjoy are priceless. After I graduated college, I flew to Florida to meet with two friends and spent a month driving across the country back to my home in California. I spent a lot of money (and trust me, I'm not a fan of spending money), but I had a blast and have no regrets. Here are a few ways to cut down on traveling costs:

By Air

Book Your Flight Early
Book your flight as early as possible and make sure to shop around. Most airlines' websites allow for instant online price quotes. There are also some great websites that search all airline flights for the cheapest ticket. Some of the more popular ones are:

www.orbitz.com	www.cheaptickets.com
www.travelocity.com	www.priceline.com

Book Your Flight Last Minute
Totally contradicting the previous paragraph, another option is to book your flight last minute. This typically works well if you have an extremely flexible schedule or you are interested in going on a vacation only if it's cheap enough. Travel agents will sometimes offer great deals on last-minute flights and total vacation packages that they were unable to sell. Check online or look in the Yellow Pages for travel agents serving your area. Ask them what last-minute deals they have available.

Standby Tickets
If you happen to know somebody who works for an airline, ask the person if he or she has any extra standby tickets. Airline employees are often given a certain number of standby tickets each year for their friends and family. The last standby ticket I used cost me $50 to fly round-trip from San Francisco to Portland. It doesn't get any cheaper than that! The only catch is that it is standby, meaning you go to the airport and cross your fingers in hopes that your flight is not full. If it is, you have to wait for the next one.

Student Deals
Many of the larger universities have a student travel center on campus. You may have graduated, but if you still have a valid student ID number or are going to graduate school, you might be able to take advantage of the

student deals the travel center offers. A few months after I graduated, I was able to get a round-trip ticket from California to Costa Rica through the student travel center for only $270—that's almost 50% less than I would have had to pay if I had gone through the airlines.

Getting Bumped

If your schedule permits it, always ask to get bumped. The airline will likely compensate you generously. The extra cost of having another passenger on an airplane is essentially just a bag of peanuts and half a drink. Therefore, airlines have a huge incentive to fill every seat and often overbook flights. If you are looking to get bumped, try to get a ticket for a flight that is almost full (the airline's web page may mention how many seats are remaining for each flight). Arrive at the boarding gate early and simply ask to be placed on the list of passengers willing to be bumped. If the flight is overbooked, they will call your name and offer you compensation to take a later flight. The compensation depends on the situation, but a typical bump would consist of a few hundred dollars in airline travel vouchers and a delay of a few hours. However, this is negotiable depending on the circumstances. The best compensation I received was for the first time I was bumped. I was delayed for one day in Hawaii in exchange for a free hotel room in Honolulu, $500 in airline travel vouchers, and a first class ticket back to California the following day. Travel vouchers often have limitations, such as expiration dates, non-transferability, and blackout dates such as Christmas, Thanksgiving, and New Years, but regardless, being bumped is a great opportunity.

Free Drinks! Whoo-hooo!

By the way, alcoholic drinks are often free on international flights and can sometimes help make the time go by faster. But don't sit in the aisle instead of your seat and don't throw peanuts at your friend a few rows up. They'll cut you off, trust me.

By Car

When I spent my month on the road after college, one thing I definitely learned was that when traveling on a budget, you have two choices: either make your trip short or sacrifice some of the normal things in life for gas money. Your choice here depends on your personality and priorities in life, but I definitely chose the latter. During the month I spent crossing the United States, my friends and I splurged on a hotel room only once and that was because we were being slowly mutilated by tiny bugs called "no-see-ums." (Don't sleep outside next to a swamp if you are ever in Florida.) Anyway, we slept most nights inside our 1990 VW Vanagon in various parking lots—yeah, we were doing the hippy thing. A campsite usually costs around $20-$25, so by sleeping in the van we saved at least $600 during the month and at least twice that much over staying in hotels.

I realize most people don't own a car they can sleep in and are forced to camp or get a hotel room. If you choose to stay in hotels, just make sure to shop around and ask for any discounts. If you're a member of AAA, you can get a discount on AAA-approved hotels by simply showing your card. As always, consider your priorities and consider the tradeoffs. Personally, if I want a nice place to stay, then I will go to my parents' house. However, if I want to experience another part of the world and enjoy time with my fellow travelers, then I prefer to get a cheap hotel or campsite. This allows me to increase the length of my stay and spend my money on experiencing the surroundings.

If you're going to camp, consider camping somewhere other than a real campsite. My friends and I have often just thrown down a tent behind some bushes in a park or on the side of the road. I would think twice about doing that in certain parts of the country, but in general, we had no problems. The worst thing that happened was being awakened by the police and told we couldn't sleep in the park—no fine, but I'm sure they could have given us one if they wanted to. As for showers, you can get them at most rest stops, campsites, or public beaches. As for food, you would be surprised how far a couple of bucks can go if your meals consist of canned food, bread, and water. You can actually have a really balanced diet that way too, believe it or not. And don't forget the free samples at Costco, Sam's Club, and grocery stores. In case you didn't know, most grocery stores allow you to sample up to three things at their deli—hit up a few grocery stores and you've got yourself a free meal.

Living this cheaply can get old and is out of the question for many people. Just keep in mind that this is only one side of the spectrum. Although I have lived that way on certain parts of a trip, I would typically find a happy medium between that and the way my parents travel. But if I had always stayed in hotels and eaten well when I traveled, the number of vacations and experiences I had would have been cut in half. Then again, if comfortable accommodations are a priority, a few quality trips may be preferable. That's your call.

Be Wary of Sales People

Purchasing certain items that we are unfamiliar with presents us with a problem: because we know too little about the subject matter to make an informed decision, we often turn to the salesperson. Although they likely understand the various options better than most people, a salesperson's suggestions are often biased and should be viewed with skepticism. Don't forget that the majority of salespeople are paid primarily with commissions and not all commissions were created equal. Depending on variables such as price, profit margin, and even just how badly the company wants to unload a certain product, commissions can vary greatly. Therefore, it is natural for the salesperson to push the product that results in the largest commission. This does not mean that all salespeople are selfish conniving bastards. You really can't blame them for this conflict of interest—it's just the way the system is set up. Salespeople are trying to get the best deal for themselves, just like you are trying to make the best purchase for yourself. So you can't really blame them, but that doesn't mean you have to be victimized by them either. Take everything they say with a grain of salt, and then analyze the purchase yourself. Salespeople are a great resource to help you acquire knowledge, but don't take their recommendations—use your newly acquired knowledge to make your own decisions. Knowledgeable friends or professionals who are not selling the product as well as consumer report-type publications are also a great resource. After you make a decision, it may be best to bypass the salesperson. Businesses appreciate it when salespeople are avoided because then commissions are also avoided. Therefore, price incentives are typically offered to customers who purchase through an alternative means, such as directly with the sales manager or through the Internet.

Keep in mind that salespeople are not limited to the 18-year-old kid at Comp USA. Real estate agents, loan agents, car salespeople, and investment brokers are all salespeople with similar conflicts of interest.

Internet Shopping

No doubt, the Internet is America's favorite shopping mall. Prices are almost always lower than those in the stores. I never buy clothing or similar items online because it's nice to try them on first, but for most other goods, buying online just makes sense. Online retailers have eliminated key expenses such as rent on retail space and paying wages to in-store employees. Therefore, it is quite easy for them to beat the prices of traditional retailers.

Since our generation grew up with the Internet, a list of online retailers seems unnecessary, but check out this one: www.shoptrc.com. It is an online retailer of computer products. An important thing to note is that the company offers discounts to students and educators. These discounts can often be massive. For example, I recently purchased an $829 package of Adobe graphics software for only $375. You may have graduated, but I'm sure you have friends or family members who are either students or educators and are therefore eligible for the discount.

Another great benefit to buying online is that if the retailer is based in a different state than your own, you don't pay sales tax. Be careful with shipping costs though. They can mount up and make purchasing online less attractive. Be especially wary on eBay. Some retailers will sell products extremely cheap, so you think you're getting an awesome deal, but then they charge ridiculously high shipping charges (e.g., a brand new DVD for $1.99 with a $15 shipping and handling charge).

Weddings

If you are presently engaged or you are "engaged to be engaged," then congratulations! I hope you have a wonderful life with your spouse and I hope I can help you save some money on the most expensive party you will probably ever throw—that's right, even more expensive than that time you splurged on a keg of Heineken in college. Luckily, there are many ways to minimize the cost and still have a beautiful wedding.

> *Invitations.* Consider making your own. It's easy to make a professional-looking invitation with today's computer programs. If you're going to have a large wedding, this can save you a relatively large amount of money.

> *Photography.* A professional photographer can be quite expensive. Instead, you could have a friend with a nice camera be the designated photographer or you could hire a student from the photography class at the local college. Another great alternative is to purchase a lot of disposable cameras and place them at each table with a note asking the guests to assist in taking pictures. This way, you will get many pictures from all different perspectives.

> *Reception Location.* This can account for a huge part of the wedding budget. Fortunately, there are many inexpensive options. If you have a family friend with a nice house and a big yard, perhaps you could have the reception there. Reserving a section of a public park or renting a city-owned recreation hall are other options.

> *Flowers.* If you decide to go with a florist, get several quotes. Prices may vary substantially. There are some other less conventional options as well. You could design your own flower arrangements by simply getting ideas from books or you could hire a starving student from the local college's horticulture program.

> *Formalwear.* I don't even own an outfit that costs $100, but recently when I was the best man for a friend's wedding, that's how much I had to pay to rent one. If you pay for all of your groomsmen's tuxedos and bridesmaid's dresses, you will have a hefty bill. It is not uncommon for these guests to pay for their own rentals or purchases.

Your wedding day is supposed to be the happiest day of you and your spouse's lives. And so as with all relationship issues, when it comes to the wedding, it is important for the two of you to communicate each of your desires and priorities to one another. Weigh the pros and cons of each cost and reach a conclusion. You definitely do not want to ruin your spouse's wedding day by being too cheap, but do consider these cost-cutting ideas. It is quite possible to have a beautiful and memorable wedding on a small budget.

Chapter 2: What It's All About

Expensive is not always better. Creativity is a superb substitute for money. Small, everyday expenses add up to a hefty sum over time and small changes in lifestyle can provide great financial benefits over the long haul.

Chapter **3**

YOUR AUTOMOBILE

Buying a Car

There are many things to consider before purchasing an automobile. First off, you need to decide which kind of car you want. Make sure to weigh all the pros and cons of each option. If you decide to go with a more expensive car, just make sure that the benefits are worth the price. I hate hearing young people argue that they bought a brand new $40,000 Chevy Tahoe because they like to snowboard and need the four-wheel-drive for the snow. If the alternative is an $18,000 Honda Civic, is it really worth $22,000 more, plus the added gas expense, just so you don't have to put chains on a few times a year and buy a roof rack? On the other hand, maybe having a cool new SUV truly makes you happy, you need to tow a boat or trailer, or you love to go off-roading. In such cases, it might be a smart decision to go with the Tahoe instead of the Civic. Just make sure you are aware of the benefits you're receiving from a certain car and that they are worth the cash you are sacrificing.

New vs. Used

Once you have decided which kind of car to buy, the biggest question is whether to buy new or used. I am a huge proponent of buying used. It makes so much more sense, especially for a young person. Generally speaking, new cars lose about 20% of their value the second you drive them off the lot. That's a lot of cash—a $30,000 car would turn into a $24,000 car before you even got a chance to enjoy owning it. There are plenty of nice-looking used cars out there so why subject yourself to such a loss? I'm not saying to buy a 1972 VW Bus (although that is a sweet van!). Just consider going a few years back so that you can avoid that ridiculous new-car depreciation rate. On the other hand, new cars are obviously less prone to mechanical problems, come with warranties, and require less shopping time, which may be important to you. Bizarre

Buying Used

The best place to shop for a used car is through the Internet. Check out websites such as www.autotraderonline.com and www.craigslist.org, or read the local newspaper's online classifieds section. Make all the phone calls, ask all the questions, and then spend some time checking out each car. Whatever you do, do not make a decision on the spot. Consider all of your options and then give yourself a day to think it over. If you have limited mechanical know-how, it is probably a good idea to get either a knowledgeable friend or a mechanic to check over the car before you purchase it. Take a test drive straight to your local mechanic. If the seller objects, there is probably something wrong with the car and you would not want to buy it anyway.

Once you decide to buy a certain car, it's time to negotiate price. Negotiation is an art form and the strategy depends on the specific situation. However, practically every seller is willing to negotiate at least a little, so don't pay the asking price. Many people like to make offers over the phone. This may save time, but you have much more power in person. When sellers take the time to show you the car and then see your cash or checkbook in hand, they get excited and are much more willing to accept an offer.

New Car Negotiation

If you decide to buy a new car, here is a process that I have found to work quite well. Using the phone book or the Internet, make a list of all dealers within at least a hundred mile radius. Before you call, make sure you know exactly which model and which options you desire. Then call each dealership and ask to speak with the fleet sales manager. During the conversation, feel free to make it known that their dealership is only one of many you are calling. They will feel the threat of competition and understand that if they do not present you with their lowest price, then you will go elsewhere. I usually say that I have about six other dealers that I am contacting. There needs to be the threat of competition, but I figure that if I say I'm calling 20 dealerships (which I am), then the competition is perceived to be so great that the dealer will not even bother with me, so I say six. Immediately following the call, fax the dealer a description of exactly what you want. They will reply with their best offer which you will compare to all the others. And don't limit yourself to local dealerships. Believe it or not, it can sometimes make financial sense to purchase a new car from a distant city and have it transported to your home on a semi-truck.

Cash vs. Financing

Now that you have found your car, you are confronted with yet another choice: cash or credit? If you don't have enough money, then obviously paying all cash is not an option. But if you don't have enough cash to purchase your chosen car, then you may want to consider a less expensive automobile. A car is a consumer good and, like all consumer purchases, it is best to avoid credit. It just doesn't make sense to buy a depreciating asset on credit. Not only are you losing something like 15% each year on the car's value, but you are also paying something like 8% each year in interest on the loan. All together, that is a lot of value that you are losing.

Dealers may offer attractive financing options such as extremely low interest rates or even 0% for the first few years of the loan. At first glance, these appear to be amazing deals, but that is often just an illusion. Try putting yourself in the dealer's shoes. Would you lend $20,000 to a stranger without being entitled to interest? Of course not. So would a dealership lend $20,000 to a stranger without being entitled to interest? Only if they were compensated by receiving a higher price. Dealers will often tell you that a car is the same price whether you pay cash or finance the purchase. This may be true when comparing an all cash deal to a standard financed deal, but I can almost guarantee that the dealer would be willing to accept a lower price for an all cash purchase compared to a 0% interest purchase.

Leasing an Automobile

As discussed in the previous section, it often makes the most sense to pay all cash for an automobile. However, this may be unrealistic for the broke recent graduate whose priorities include driving a cool car. Assuming this is the case, you basically have two options: You can either finance your purchase with an automobile loan or you can lease the car. With a loan, you make monthly payments for a period of time until the car is fully paid off and then the car is yours. But how does a lease work? With a lease, you also have a down payment and regular monthly payments, but unlike the loan, once the lease expires, the car belongs to the dealer. Leases are attractive to consumers because they tend to have lower monthly payments compared to loans. However, look at the main difference between leasing vs. financing: After the lease ends, you own absolutely nothing. This is a big difference and explains the lower monthly payments on a lease. So, which is better—a loan or a lease? Unfortunately, you need to do a little analysis. Once you have decided on the make and model, get quotes from various dealers for both loans and leases. Take the most favorable loan and the most favorable lease and analyze them. Use the following example as a guide for your analysis.

Loan / Lease Analysis

	Fin		
1	e Price		18,000
2	Do ent		2,500
3	Sales		8%
4	Sales tax × 3)	$	1,440
5	Term of Loan ase (in years)		3
6	Term of Loan a (in months		36
7	Monthly Payment	$	485
8	Total payments (items	$	17,460
9	Savings account interest		3%
10	Opportunity cost of do ms 2 × 5 × 9)	$	225
11	Estimated value of e end an	$	9,000
12	**Total Cost of F (item 2 + 0 - 11)**	$	**12,625**

Leasing

13	yment		500
14	y Payment		365
	al payments (items 6 × 14)	$	0
	Opportunity cost of down payment (items 5 × 9 × 13)	$	
	Total Cost of Leasing (items 13 + 15 + 16)	$	**13,**

OK, I lied. No analysis. In the interest of avoiding your rebellious act of flushing this book down the toilet while violently cursing and flailing your arms about, I omitted the boring number-crunching analysis. Just take my word for it that, as a general rule, leasing is the more costly option. It does allow you to have lower monthly payments for a given car or allow you to have a more expensive car for a given monthly payment, but this is a narrow view. You need to consider the fact that with a loan, you actually own the car, which is a huge benefit. With a lease, you own nothing. So, yes, leases have lower monthly payments, but, overall, they are the more expensive option.

Sell It Yourself or Trade It In?

When it comes time to make peace and say goodbye to that old car, you will be posed with two options: trade it in to a dealer or sell it yourself. As far as straight finances go, the choice is simple—sell it yourself. A dealer will turn around and sell your car for about the same price that you could sell it for in the classifieds, but because they need to account for advertising, rent, commissions, and profit, you will receive a highly discounted price for your car. Kelly Blue Book estimates that the price difference between trade-in and private party values for a Honda Accord, for example, is $2,130. That's a decent chunk of cash you might prefer to have in your pocket instead of in the used car dealer's pocket.

Of course, there are reasons to consider trading your old car to a dealer, such as the undeniable convenience. If you are short on time and don't want to deal with the hassles involved with selling, then you may want to accept a discounted price in exchange for a quick, easy sale. Also, if your budget is tight and you choose to sell your car yourself, you may be car-less for a period of time between the car sale and the new car purchase. This can be avoided by trading in your car, which allows you to simultaneously purchase your new car and sell the old one.

Chapter 3: What It's All About

Car loans and particularly car leases tend to be more expensive overall compared to a cash purchase. New cars have extraordinarily high depreciation rates. Make sure to shop around whether you are buying used or new.

Chapter **4**

GETTING ORGANIZED

Financial Goal Setting

At the heart of every person's financial situation are their goals. These goals may be significant and long-term, such as buying a home, retiring comfortably, or paying for graduate school. Or they may be as simple as going on a weekend vacation. The first step to creating a financial plan, or any plan for that matter, is to establish and define these goals, both big and small, long term and short term. Try this out. Later on tonight, lay in bed and take some time to consider exactly what you want out of life and scribble it down on a piece of paper. You may want to include both financial goals as well as other personal or social goals, but we will focus on the financial ones here. The more specific you are, the better. For example, don't just say you want to be rich, because this can mean different things to different people. To you, rich may mean having $5 million, but someone else may consider having $500,000 as being rich. Instead, try being more specific, like saying, "I want to have a net worth of $250,000 by the age of 30." Now, after you have completed your list, try to prioritize by organizing the list with the most important goals at the top and the least important at the bottom. It would probably be useful to rank each goal on an importance scale of 1 to 10 before reorganizing the list. Then, next to each goal, write down the time period you are giving yourself to achieve this goal and the total cost of the goal. You may also want to create separate lists for short-term and long-term goals. This is a very subjective task and the order as well as the goals themselves will likely change every year if not every day, which is fine. You can revise your list as needed.

Compare your financial plan to a road trip. Consider your list of goals as your destinations. When on a road trip, the first thing you need to know is where you are going and then you need to prioritize your destinations because it would take a lifetime to visit every place across the continent. You might sacrifice visiting Bubba's Shrimp Shack in order to see the Florida Keys, just like you might sacrifice buying new jeans in order to save for a car. Besides destinations, the other main part of a road trip is a road map. You may know where you are going, but you also need to know how you are going to get there. That's where the rest of this book comes in, which you may consider a financial road map to wherever your destinations may be. But first things first—you need those destinations.

Budgeting

Budgeting is often heavily preached when it comes to personal finance. Although it is usually quite effective in forcing savings and eliminating credit card debt, I have to admit that I am not a big fan. I feel like the whole budgeting concept is too restrictive, at least when properly adhered to. Under the typical budgeting strategy, a certain dollar limit is created for each expense category for a certain time period and you don't allow yourself to exceed that limit. It can work quite well and might be a great idea for some people. Personally though, I don't want my life to be that structured. I don't like to constantly worry about keeping every expense within the budgeted amount. Instead of the typical budgeting process, I prefer to simply keep track of my expenses each month and then periodically reflect on them to see if my spending behavior needs to be altered. I guess it's actually quite similar to budgeting, just a little less restrictive. It gives me a certain piece of mind to know where everything is and where everything went. It also gives me some insight into how certain life changes will affect me. For example, if I ever want to take time off from work to take care of a child, go back to school, or pursue some other interest, I would have a good idea of how much money I would need each month and therefore whether or not I would have sufficient savings to handle the lifestyle change.

If you do want to make a budget or at least keep track of your income and expenses, I recommend that you use a computer program. For basic budgeting and expense records, Microsoft Excel works fine. However, if you really want to get into it, I recommend you use a program such as Quicken or Microsoft Money. These programs can do just about anything that you would want in regards to organizing your finances. One really cool thing about them is that they can easily download your account balances through the Internet and reflect the changes in all your financial statements and graphs. Although these programs may be unnecessary at this stage in your life, they can become extremely useful as you get older and your financial situation gets more complicated.

Financial Offense vs. Defense

Accumulating wealth in life is a game. Like any game, there are offensive and defensive moves. If you focus too much on one and ignore the other, you will likely lose the game. In the game of accumulating wealth, saving money is the defense and earning income and investing is the offense. Unfortunately, many people focus too much on one side and not the other. At one extreme, you have the offensive player, such as the stereotypical doctor who makes a lot of money but then spends every penny on fancy cars, gourmet dinners, and all the latest technology. At the other extreme, you have the cheap idiot who swims through fountains at Disneyland in pursuit of shiny nickels. He spends so much time trying to save money that he forgets to make any. Many defensive players will spend an hour to save $5. Where is the logic in that? After all, your time is worth something and if you value your time at your wage rate, then you are essentially spending somewhere around $25 in order to save $5. I would think that most people value their time at more than $5/hour. If that hour was taken away from defense and used towards offense, then the $5 would be lost but $25 would be made, so you would be $20 better off.

Both offense and defense are important, but that does not imply equal efforts in both areas. You need to weigh the pros and cons and consider the tradeoffs between each offensive and defensive move. In the above example, it probably makes sense to apply that hour towards offense if an hour of defense will only save you $5. However, if the hour could have been spent arguing a car insurance claim, which could save you $100, then it may be smarter to focus on that defensive move instead of an offensive one. When examples like these are laid out clearly, the answers seem obvious—and they often are. However, the problem arises in forcing yourself to think about which moves (offensive or defensive) make the most sense at a certain time, and that is something that few people consistently do.

Bank Accounts

When it comes to opening up a bank account, there are numerous options to choose from. First off, which bank deserves the honor of protecting your money? I prefer going with a large bank with many branches. I tend to leave town fairly often and like knowing that I can always find a branch of my bank. Because of the size and efficiency of the larger institutional banks, these banks also have the ability to provide very competitive services at low costs. At the other end of the spectrum are local banks, which are often owned by members of the community. These community banks are naturally much smaller and therefore more inefficient, which results in slightly higher costs. However, without as many corporate regulations, they are often better at catering to the personal situations of individuals and small businesses. This might come in handy when it comes to more complicated issues such as applying for a home loan. However, when it comes to basic banking (i.e., checking accounts), I prefer the larger national banks.

Credit Unions

Another possible option is a credit union. A credit union offers the same services as a traditional bank. The main difference is that credit unions are non-profit organizations that provide banking services to their members. There are often requirements to joining a credit union, such as belonging to a certain group or working for a certain employer. If you are eligible, credit unions tend to provide great service at a low cost, and might make a lot of sense for you. However, similar to small local banks, they lack the geographical dispersion of larger banking institutions, which could be an inconvenience if you leave town often.

Internet Banking

Banking over the Internet is a relatively new yet exciting option. It is often accompanied by a standard checking account from a traditional bank. Since, Internet banks have no branch offices, they are able to offer extremely competitive rates. Check out www.INGDirect.com or www. EmigrantDirect.com, for example. These Internet banks tend to offer rates on savings accounts that are substantially higher than that of traditional banks.

Here's how it works. You have a free checking account from Washington Mutual and then you also sign up for an ING Direct Internet savings account. When you have depleted your Washington Mutual checking account, you simply log on to ING's website and transfer money to your checking account. This transfer usually takes a few days.

Banking Fees

Whatever form of bank you choose, the important thing is that you don't pay fees. Savings and checking accounts provide banks the means to issue loans for a profit. They pay a low interest rate on their customers' deposits and then charge a higher interest rate on their loans. The difference, or spread as it is commonly referred to, is where their profit comes from. Without your deposits, there would be no profit. You are helping them out and so you shouldn't stand for paying fees.

The best banking advice I can give you is to not be loyal to any one bank. If another bank is offering a better deal, notify your bank and if they don't match it, close your account. Your relationship with a bank is not a friendship, there's no reason for loyalty. The bank is in the business of making money and you are in the business of protecting your money, so follow the good deals.

By the way, a little tip in case you don't already know it: a few banks, Washington Mutual, for one, do not charge a fee for using their ATMs even if you do not have an account with them. So if you can't find an ATM for your own bank, feel free to use theirs.

MMAs

MMA stands for money market account, and these can be great alternatives to keeping money in a savings account. Like a savings account, you have access to your money market account at any time. The difference lies in the intended use of the funds. Money in a savings account is lent out to customers in the form of personal and home loans, whereas money in a money market account is invested in short-term debt securities, such as U.S. Treasury Bills. You can essentially think of MMAs as savings accounts on steroids.

The interest rate on these accounts is variable and depends on the corresponding short-term debt market interest rates. However, with a long-term average around 5%, it is often significantly higher than the interest rates earned on savings accounts. Another great benefit to MMAs is that most of them allow for check-writing privileges as long as the checks are written for an amount greater than a specified minimum (currently $250 with Vanguard Accounts). As long as the corresponding minimum balance is reasonable for your situation, a money market account could be a great alternative to a savings or checking account and should definitely at least be considered. Go to www.bankrate.com to check out what's available out there.

Identity Theft

Identity theft is the fastest growing crime in the United States. It occurs when somebody obtains your personal information and uses it to commit financial fraud. If left unnoticed, it can become a huge problem. The following are a few of the many possible methods that identity thieves may use:

> They may open new credit card accounts in your name and not pay them off.

> They may write bad checks on a bank account opened in your name.

> They may purchase an automobile on credit in your name and not pay it off.

> They may give your name and info to the police during an arrest and ditch out on their court date, resulting in a warrant being issued for your arrest.

> They may file fraudulent tax forms in your name.

> They may file for bankruptcy in your name.

> They may get a driver's license with your name and their picture.

All of the previous scenarios can result in severe financial problems for the victim. Governmentguide.com provides the following tips to help prevent identity theft:

How To Prevent Identity Theft

> ➤ Shred all credit card, bank and other financial statements.

> ➤ Always use secure Web sites for Internet purchases.

> ➤ Do not discuss financial matters on wireless or cellular phones.

> ➤ Write or call your Motor Vehicles Dept. to have your personal information protected from disclosure.

> ➤ Do not use your mother's maiden name as a password on your credit cards.

> ➤ Be wary of anyone calling to "confirm" personal information.

> ➤ Thoroughly review all bank, credit card and phone statements for unusual activity.

> ➤ Monitor when new credit cards, checks or ATM cards are being mailed to you and report any that are missing or late.

> ➤ Close all unused credit and bank accounts, destroy old credit cards and shred unused credit card offers.

> ➤ Remove your Social Security number from checks, driver's licenses or other identification.

> ➤ Always ask for the carbon papers of credit purchases.

> ➤ Do not leave outgoing credit card payments in your mailbox.

> ➤ Do not carry your Social Security card in your wallet unless needed.

> ➤ ORDER YOUR CREDIT REPORT ONCE A YEAR AND LOOK FOR ANOMALIES.

The most important tip above is to check your credit at least once a year. If you have been victimized by identity thieves, this is where you'll find out. It's quite easy to do. Just go to www.freecreditreport.com.

Chapter 4: What It's All About
Throughout life, goals should be defined, reflected upon, and revised as needed. Every decision we make should in some way or another contribute to achieving these goals. This is the best way to ensure a successful future.

Chapter 5

CONSUMER CREDIT

Why to Avoid Credit Card Debt

Credit card debt is one of the most common financial burdens facing recent graduates. Although credit cards can be great money management tools when used responsibly, their use by many young adults is anything but responsible. It feels like you're getting free stuff – you don't have to hand over actual money and you don't even have to pay the credit card company back until you feel like it. Credit cards offer the ability to live well beyond your means, which can result in disastrous levels of debt. To make matters even worse, this debt is compounded by a ridiculous interest rate, as high as 20% on some credit cards.

According to a recent survey, the average college senior has roughly $2,800 in credit card debt. Let's say that this average student graduates and begins to pay the debt off. Assuming he only makes the minimum payments and has a 15% interest rate, it will take him almost 30 years to pay it all off. In the end, assuming she did not rack up more debt, she will pay a total of approximately $7,000 for a $2,800 original balance. This is outrageous! Each one of those $6 Chipotle burritos actually costs $15! Knowing this in advance would cause most people to think twice about racking up such debt.

So now you know how important it is to avoid credit card debt, but what about those of you who have already fallen victim to the shiny plastic demons? The advice here is simple: Pay it off as quickly as possible! Paying off your debt and avoiding the ridiculously high interest charges is perhaps the best investment that you could make.

Avoiding Interest on Credit Card Debt

Although the previous situation is a reality for many young Americans, credit card debt does not have to be that threatening to your bank account. I offer you the following tip not as an excuse to accumulate debt but as a method to minimize the interest expense <u>while you pay off your debt.</u> Don't try to convince yourself that just because you can avoid interest, it is OK to rack up credit card debt. Spending all that cash still prevents future investment and, as your debt grows, your ability to achieve future goals, such as buying a home, dwindles. That being said, here's how to avoid paying interest on your balance.

There are many credit cards available that offer 0% interest rates on balance transfers. These are meant to be teaser rates to attract business. Six to eighteen months later, the credit card company will raise the interest rates through the roof. In many cases, you can transfer your existing debt balance to these cards, pay nothing in interest, and then right before the 0% interest rate deal expires, you can transfer the balance to a different 0% interest deal. If you have existing credit card debt, you can greatly benefit from this "scam," but do so with caution. Make sure to read the fine print. Remember that credit card companies are a business and need to make money, so there is always some kind of catch. In many cases there is a phrase that declares any payments made on the account go towards paying down the existing debt instead of any new debt. Therefore, if you make purchases on the card, you will still get the 0% rate on the balance transfer but will be forced to pay a high interest rate on any new debt. All payments will be applied against the original balance first, so you will continue to pay interest on new debt until the entire balance is paid off. To avoid this problem, you should have one 0% credit card allocated for existing debt and a separate card for everyday purchases. There are also many credit cards that offer 0% interest rates on new purchases.

Take advantage of these opportunities, but again, READ THE FINE PRINT. As my Dad would say, "Know the rules of the game before playing. Otherwise you're just an idiot running in a circle." I think he was talking about baseball. Anyway, check out www.bankrate.com for information on what credit card deals are currently available. Or just open up your mailbox and you'll probably have several pieces of junk mail credit card offers to choose from.

Managing Your Debt

When it comes to managing credit card debt, there's really not much advice to be given. The concept is simple—just pay it off! However, the issue is not necessarily how to manage the debt, but rather how to manage yourself.

It's really about self-discipline. The first step is to get your spending habits under control – cut up all your credit cards, don't step foot into a shopping mall, and don't browse eBay. Avoid putting yourself in situations where you know you can't help but buy, buy, buy. After you have curbed your frivolous spending habits, it's time to pay off your debt. The key to achieving this is to simply make it a priority. Make the payment at a standard time each month when you know you'll have money, such as after you receive your paycheck. You should always make the credit card payment first. If you have money left over for entertainment, clothes, etc., then great, but if you don't, then you'll have to hold off on these luxuries. We all want to have fun with our money, but by paying off credit card debt you are allowing yourself to have much more fun with money in the future. Paying interest on credit card debt is probably the least fun way to spend money, as it is just a hole in your wallet and provides nothing in return. In summary, paying interest on a credit card is about as fun as having hemorrhoids, so eat your fiber and pay off your debt.

The amount you allocate towards paying off your debt each month is up to you, but I would encourage you to pay as much as possible. Credit card interest rates are often ridiculously high and you would greatly benefit from avoiding that expense. Also, an important thing to realize is that by only making the minimum payment, you really aren't doing anything to rid yourself of your debt. As previously discussed, the minimum payment is structured in such a way so that it could take you close to 30 years to pay it off.

The Effect of Consumer Debt on a Home Purchase

Saving to purchase your first home is arguably the best financial decision you can make at your age. However, your ability to accomplish this goal can be hindered by your abuse of consumer credit. Banks only want to lend money if they believe the borrower to be capable of meeting the payment schedule. Therefore, banks only allow a specified percentage of your gross income to be allocated towards debt payments. Therefore, if your income is somewhat limited (as is the case for most recent grads), any consumer debt could prevent you from qualifying for the home loan that you are relying on. Let's look at an example.

Let's say that you graduated last year and landed a job earning $48,000 a year, or $4,000 a month. Assuming the bank allows 40% of your gross income to be allocated towards all debt payments and you have no other debt, $1,600 of that monthly income can be allocated towards a mortgage payment. With an 8% annual interest rate and a 30-year loan, that monthly payment would correspond to a $218,000 loan.

Now let's assume that you have monthly payments of $500 because of some sort of consumer debt—a car loan, for example. You can still allocate $1,600 towards debt payments, but since you already have $500 in monthly payments, you can only allocate the remaining $1,100 towards your mortgage payment. Under the same assumptions as above (8%, 30-year loan), you can now only qualify for a $150,000 home loan. That's $68,000 less than if you didn't have the car loan!

If you didn't follow all that number crunching, don't worry about it. Just know that consumer debt substantially decreases a person's ability to purchase real estate and that this decrease in borrowing power is often enough to prevent a home purchase altogether. If you are planning on purchasing your first house soon, avoid a bad surprise by being aware of this rule. Hopefully, you will be able to pay off any consumer debt and still have enough cash left over to make a down payment.

Note that payments on student loans impact your home purchase in the same way. However, student loans often have low interest rates and a prolonged payback period, which minimizes their effect on borrowing power when compared to consumer debt such as a car loan. Also, from a financial point of view, borrowing money for education is undoubtedly a better use of credit than purchasing a new Lexus.

Chapter 5: What It's All About

Avoid consumer debt at all costs. There is absolutely nothing beneficial to such liabilities. Credit cards may be terrific cash management tools, but there is an evil gremlin lurking inside that shiny plastic ready to inject you with 19% interest rates as soon as a balance is not paid in full.

Chapter **6**

GENERAL INVESTING

Now that real life is beginning and money is slowly but surely accumulating (right?), you need a plan for that money. Simply earning a salary and setting aside savings is not enough—it is important that you invest that savings. Proper investing can make a remarkably large difference in a person's financial well-being and it is therefore one of the most important subjects in personal finance. Good investment techniques have been known to make the poorly paid high school teacher one of the richest guys in town, while poor investment decisions can cause the highly paid doctor to become the poorest dude in town.

This book is but a mere introduction to the investment world and I encourage you to pursue greater knowledge on this topic. Nonetheless, I believe the following discussion to be extremely beneficial to recent graduates who are preparing to enter the investment world.

Know Yourself Before You Invest

Before investing your hard-earned cash, it is important to take a step back and analyze your personality. Knowing yourself—what you like, don't like, and how you feel about things—is always beneficial as it allows you to direct your life in a positive direction. When it comes to finances, particularly investing and insurance, it is very important to confront yourself with the question: How do I feel about risk? Many of the financial decisions you will make come down to how you answer this question. Do you invest in risky speculative assets such as the South African stock market or in extremely safe U.S. Treasury Inflation-Protected Securities? Do you pay extra for collision on your auto insurance policy or do you take the chance of driving without it in hopes that you won't crash? Do you take that shady tax deduction and risk being audited or do you ignore it to avoid IRS nightmares? Know how you feel about risk and you will have the answers to all these sort of questions. It might not make sense for you to take some of my advice on how to save or make more money if it is going to result in anxiety. Some people can handle risk and others cannot. Wherever you stand is fine as long as you live accordingly. If you don't mind risk, then make those risky investments and you will likely be rewarded in the long term. But if risk bothers you, take a more conservative approach to investing and you'll live longer.

But how exactly do you know if risk bothers you? This is an extremely subjective issue and there are many questionnaires available to analyze the issue. But perhaps the best way to determine a person's risk tolerance is by answering a single question: Would you prefer to have a guaranteed $400 or flip a coin with heads earning you $1,000 and tails earning zero dollars? If you weren't already aware of your feelings towards risk, answer this question and you will know.

Sexy Investments

Sexy investments are those that are exciting to the investor. Such investments tend to provide minimal profits for a simple reason: supply and demand. If everyone wants to buy a certain investment because it is exciting, then the demand for that investment rises. With an increased demand, the price would naturally rise and people would pay more for the same investment, resulting in minimal profits.

Consider an unattractive investment: a waste management business. Did you know that this industry tends to be highly profitable? Garbage is gross, dirty, and not the least bit exciting. It is not a sexy business. Why would anyone want to own or invest in a waste management business? An opportunistic business person would likely be attracted to this business because everyone else finds it so unappealing. Opportunity often arises in places where people either have not looked or, in this case, don't want to look. The waste management industry is unattractive to most people, resulting in minimal competition and maximum profit potential.

Now let us consider a sexy industry: entertainment, or actors, to be specific. And no, I'm not talking about the Brad Pitts and Jennifer Anistons of the world. For every Brad Pitt there are probably a hundred or more struggling actors in Los Angeles who are just trying to make ends meet. So why are these actors struggling so much? Because there is so much damn competition. Everyone and their mother dreams of being an actor or actress. Again, it goes back to supply and demand—with such a large supply of actors, the price of an actor (i.e. the actor's salary) is bound to be minimal. There is no need to pay them too much because there will always be another actor waiting in line to get a shot at his big debut. This example may refer more to career, but the same is true of investments. Popularity and excitement for a particular investment tend to increase the price of that investment even though the actual investment quality remains unchanged. The result is nothing more than an attractive pile of junk.

The opposite can be true of non-sexy and downright boring investments. Since no one cares to buy them, their price is often lower, resulting in an even more profitable investment. My point is simple—there is opportunity and profit to be had in sectors of the economy that others have neglected. I'm not saying that you or I should necessarily pursue these kinds of opportunities because we may be emotionally better off neglecting them as well, despite the profit potential. There is often a good reason why others have not pursued such opportunities and it is important to understand why before jumping on board. There are always tradeoffs involved. Like anything, weigh the pros and cons and then make the decision that is right for you.

Investment Types

There are many different types of investments out there—some are self-explanatory and others are more confusing. A 500-page book could be written about each one of these investments, so my brief descriptions are not likely to do them justice. Nevertheless, it is important to at least get acquainted with the various options, so here are some basic descriptions of the more common investments:

Stocks: The fractional ownership of a company.

> ➢ *Large-Cap U.S. Stocks:* Large-cap stands for large capitalization, which implies that these stocks represent ownership of big corporations that make up a relatively large portion of the overall stock market. Examples would be Ford Motor, Microsoft, and Coca-Cola. The S&P 500 is an index that tracks the 500 largest companies on the U.S. market and is often used as a measure of the stock market as a whole. Because large-cap stocks are all very established companies,

they tend to be much safer investments than the smaller unknown companies.

> *Small-Cap U.S. Stocks:* Of course, these are smaller less-known companies in the market. Because they are often less established, they tend to be riskier than large-cap stocks and therefore have higher average returns. At the extreme end of the small-cap spectrum lies penny stocks, which can literally be priced as low as a penny/share. These are extremely risky and should be avoided by most investors, although if you have a Vegas-like personality, they can also be quite fun. It is much easier to double your money in penny stocks. You don't see a $50 stock rise to $100 overnight, but it's quite common to see a 20 cent stock rise to 40 cents or more overnight. On the other hand, it's also quite common and probably more likely to see penny stocks fall to zero cents.

> *Mid-Cap U.S. Stocks:* These are everything in between large-cap and small-cap stocks.

> *International Stocks:* These investments can be either relatively stable (e.g., European markets) or extremely risky (e.g., South American markets). International stocks can be a great way to diversify a portfolio without sacrificing expected returns.

Bonds: When you invest in a bond, you are basically loaning money to a corporation or governmental agency. Bonds usually come in one of two forms. The first form is a coupon bond, on which interest payments are made twice a year and the initial amount loaned is paid back upon expiration. With coupon bonds, you might loan $1,000 in the form of a bond, then receive $50 dollars every six months for five years. At the end of five years, you would also receive the $1,000 that was initially loaned. The other form is a zero-coupon bond, on which no interest payments are made and instead, one large lump-sum payment is made upon the bond's expiration. You might pay $1,000 for a zero-coupon bond and not receive anything until several years later, when you get $1,600. Bonds can also have several options embedded in their contracts. Examples include convertible bonds (the bonds can be converted to stock), callable bonds (the borrower has the option to buy back the bonds from the investor at a specified price), and putable bonds (the bond investor has the option to sell back or redeem the bonds at a specified price).

> ➤ *Treasury Notes and Bonds:* Treasury notes have maturity periods between 1 and 10 years and treasury bonds have maturities of 30 years. Both are sold in $1,000 increments and are backed by the good faith of the federal government.

> ➤ *Treasury Bills:* Short-term debt of the federal government. You have the choice of 13-, 26-, or 52-week maturity periods. Like most debt securities, Treasury Bills (also called T-Bills) come in $1,000 increments.

> ➤ *Inflation Indexed Treasury Notes and Bonds:* The interest rate on these bonds is tied to inflation. If inflation is high, then the interest rate on these bonds is high, but if inflation is low, then so is the interest rate. This offers great inflation protection and is therefore often attractive to older retirees who are more vulnerable to inflation.

> ➤ *Corporate Bonds:* Corporations have two ways of raising money: They can issue stock or they can issue bonds. When you own stock in a company, you actually own a piece of the company. You completely share its risks and its profits. When you own a corporate bond, you do not own any part of the company. Instead you simply have an IOU, with the company's assets as collateral. The corporate bond market is very broad and the bonds vary greatly in their structure and risk. There are also multiple rating agencies, such as Standard & Poor's or Moody's, which assess the risk of each bond and rate them on a sliding scale.

> ➤ *Municipal Bonds:* These are bonds issued by states, counties, parishes, cities, and towns. The unique feature of these bonds is that they are exempt from federal income tax. In many cases, they are exempt from state income taxes as well. The interest rate paid on these bonds is less than that of other bonds with similar risks. The lower interest rate accounts for the tax benefits. Investors are willing to receive less interest, because the interest income they receive is tax free. There

are two main types of municipal bonds: general obligation and revenue bonds. General obligation bonds are backed by the taxing power of the municipality and therefore have minimum risk. If money is short, the municipality can just raise taxes to pay off the bonds. Revenue bonds are used to fund specific projects and are secured only by the revenue from those specific projects. If the project does poorly, the bonds may not be repaid in full.

Mortgages: We typically associate banks with mortgages. However, individuals can issue mortgages as well. You can issue a new mortgage or purchase an existing one through the classifieds or a broker. When issued by an individual rather than a bank, a mortgage is often referred to as a trust deed. Each mortgage is unique as it corresponds to a unique piece of property, which must be analyzed in order to determine the risk of the specific mortgage. Since this is a relatively unorganized market, it is possible to find opportunities to earn excessive profits. However, you need to know what you are doing.

Certificates of Deposit: Also called CDs, these are basically deposits with a banking institution that cannot be touched for a specified amount of time. As compensation for loaning your money to the bank, you are paid a specified interest rate. Under normal circumstances, the longer you allow the bank to have your money, the higher the interest rate will be. If you withdraw your deposit before the specified time period is up, you are subject to a stiff penalty, so make sure you do not need access to that money for the specified period.

Real Estate: If approached with the right amount of care, real estate can provide relatively stable and large profits. In my opinion, this is by far the most intriguing and profitable investment category. More on real estate in Chapter 8.

Mutual Funds: Most of us associate mutual funds with the stock market. Although the stock market is typically what people refer to when they talk about mutual funds, the term is actually very general and really refers to any investment company that invests in various assets on behalf of its shareholders and then sells stock in the company. So if you buy equity mutual funds, you are investing in the stock market. If you buy bond mutual funds, you are investing in the bond market, and if you buy a money market mutual fund, then you are investing in short-term debt securities such as U.S. Treasury Bills. In fact, there is a mutual fund for just about any investment category.

Gold, Silver, Diamonds, etc.: Yeah…you're on your own here. To me, gold, silver, and diamonds represent confusion during the Holiday season when I find myself spending ridiculous amounts of cash on tiny little rocks that for some unknown reason cause women to smile. But I guess the smile alone is worth the money. I have never considered these purhcases as investments though, and doubt that I ever will. They may make terrific retail businesses, but in the end, they are consumer goods. To simply purchase these gems or metals in hopes that they will appreciate at a rate that significantly exceeds inflation seems irrational, but that's just my opinion.

Antiques and Collectibles: Unless you have real expertise, these kinds of investments tend to be more time consuming than profitable. In my humble opinion, holding onto a bunch of junk for a number of years in order to make $50 is definitely not worth it; in many cases, there is no profit. I've been waiting the past 10 years for my Joe Montana rookie football card to increase in value and I've seen nothing. I would have been much better off if I had never purchased it—although I was the coolest 14-year-old on the block for a while. Anyway, if you enjoy having certain collectibles, by all means buy them. Collecting can be a great hobby and selling collectibles can be a good business, but I would be very skeptical about calling such purchases investments. However, I have very limited knowledge in the antique/collectible markets and I expect them to be relatively inefficient, so perhaps there are profits to be had. In my experience though, the limited profits available do not nearly outweigh the hassles involved.

So which of all these investments is right for you? Take a look at your personality and specific financial situation in order to decide which investments are suitable for you. Just remember that it is important to choose more than one kind of investment. Why? Because …

Diversify, Diversify, Diversify

"Don't put all your eggs in one basket." We've all heard this saying and, if you understand it, then you understand diversification. Consider what would happen if all your investments were in one basket and the basket broke. You'd be financially screwed. This may be an obvious lesson, yet it is also an extremely important one and one that, unfortunately, is often ignored. There are two levels of diversification: diversification within an investment category and portfolio-level diversification.

Diversification within an Investment Category
The cliché textbook example describes an investor with a portfolio of two stocks: an umbrella company and a sunscreen company, both of which are equally profitable. During rainy weather, the umbrella company provides great returns to the investor, yet the sunscreen company struggles. When the sun comes out, the reverse occurs: the umbrella company struggles and the sunscreen company kicks butt. As a diversified investor, the weather change has no affect on you—whatever weather the future holds, you will be financially secure. It's true that in the end you would receive the same amount of profit from either stock. However, with diversification, your profits are consistent all the way along.

To be sufficiently diversified though, you of course need more than just two stocks. Keep in mind that the types of investments are of particular importance. Having your eggs in many baskets is not the only requirement— the baskets must be significantly different from each other. For example, investing in 50 different automotive companies is not considered efficient diversification because those investments tend to fluctuate together. It's important to choose investments that have little relation to one another. For example, a stock portfolio of Krispy Kreme Donuts, Microsoft, General Motors, Albertsons, Target, and Exxon is well diversified. Diversification can be easily accomplished with a mutual fund.

Portfolio-Level Diversification
The preceding paragraph described the importance of diversification within a particular investment category (i.e. stocks). However, it is also very important to diversify on a macro or portfolio level. When developing your

portfolio, you don't want all your money in any single investment category. For example, if you had all your money in the stock market, a market crash would crush your entire portfolio. Similarly, if you had all your money in bonds and interest rates rise (which decreases the value of bonds), your entire portfolio would lose value. Luckily, these sorts of risks can be greatly reduced through diversification. By investing in various investments that have little or no correlation with one another, the ups and downs of each investment category tend to cancel each other out, resulting in greater stability and consistent investment growth. For example, if the stock market crashes, then interest rates will likely be lowered to stimulate the economy, resulting in profits for bond investors. So you lose money in the stock market, but make it in the bond market. If there is high inflation, the bond market will perform poorly, but the real estate market will skyrocket, so again, you lose money in one place but make it in another. These types of scenarios are actually quite common in the investment world and so the diversified investor is much better equipped to withstand the economic surprises that may otherwise crush her.

Your Diversification Options

There are many different ways to diversify one's portfolio; the following is a partial list of investment options. Mutual funds are available for each of these investment categories. Check out an investment broker such as Vanguard or Fidelity for a detailed description on each fund.

- U.S. Stocks
- Emerging Markets
- Real Estate Investment Trusts
- Municipal Bonds
- European Stocks
- Money Market
- Corporate Bonds
- Treasury Bonds

Now the question is: How much diversification and with which investments? You should almost always diversify within a particular investment category. So if you are going to invest in the European Stock Market, for example, buy a diversified mutual fund. However, the diversification of your portfolio as a whole is up for discussion. You will need to weigh the same tradeoffs that are always involved in personal finance: expose yourself to more risk in exchange for higher potential gains or pass up the high potential gains but minimize risk. Only you can answer this question, as the answer depends on your personality and risk tolerance. Keep in mind, though, that at your stage in life, it does make sense to invest a larger portion of your portfolio in riskier investments such as the stock market, real estate, and maybe some corporate bonds. Because of your young age and the many years you have ahead, you can easily handle the ups and downs of risky investments. Hypothetically, all investment categories have positive returns in the long run. Risky investments are really only risky in the short term. Check out the graph below:

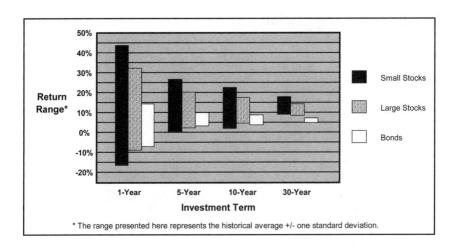

* The range presented here represents the historical average +/- one standard deviation.

Looking at the above graph, you can see how unpredictable the returns from risky investments (e.g., small stocks) can be over a short period, such as a year. However, check out the 30-year column. The return range has been substantially reduced and now the expected annual return range is 9% to 17%. Compare this to the return range of the "less risky" bonds, which have a range of about 5% to 7%. Sure, bonds have a narrower range than small stocks, but the high end of the bond's return range is only 7% while the low end of the small stock's range is 9%. What this tells us is that, in the long run, riskier investments are actually less risky. Is that a contradiction or what? Think about it though—when people refer to investment risk, they are typically referring to risk over a short time period such as a year. When you consider a long period, such as 30 years, losses in one year are offset by profits in future years. Returns are averaged out and the range narrows around the expected return, which is higher than that of the less risky investments. You have your entire life to recover from any potential financial problems, so it makes sense to be an aggressive investor at this age. At the other end of the spectrum are retirees who may not have 30 years left to ride out any financial mishaps and are therefore much more concerned with short-term risk. Unless you are extremely risk averse or have important plans for your money in the near future, most investment advisors would agree that an aggressive strategy such as stocks is right for you.

An Allocation Suggestion

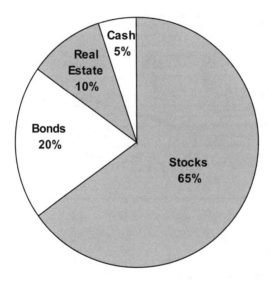

Keep in mind that this is only a suggestion and no generalization can really be made. Like all things, it depends on your situation and some modifications may be necessary. For example, I feel very comfortable with risk, so I have opted to ignore the bond market. Instead I have increased my allocations to the stock market with a significant portion in venture capital, which can be very risky. As for the real estate market, you may be wondering how to allocate 10% of your savings if you have little money. The answer lies with REITs (Real Estate Investment Trusts), which are explained later on in this book.

Large Profits and No Risk?

Yeah, you wish! There is no such thing as a free lunch. We have all heard that saying many times before about all aspects of life investing is no different. If you want to make big money, you will have to risk something. There are three main methods of maximizing investment profits:

1. Time

Give up access to your investment for a lengthy time period and risk your money not being accessible when you need it. For example, an investor will receive a higher interest rate on a 20-year bond versus a 5-year bond.

2. Loss of Investment

Expose yourself to the risk of losing your investment. Investments such as the stock market tend to be very volatile and you could lose a good portion of your investment. However, over the long haul, the average returns on "high-risk" investments are much higher than other less volatile investments.

3. Headaches

Expose yourself to the risk of massive ongoing headaches. With certain investments such as real estate and other entrepreneurial efforts, unforeseen problems seem to attack you from every direction and can be very stressful for some people. In exchange for taking on this burden, investors will often be rewarded by the market with higher returns.

A common measure of risk for a particular investment is its standard deviation. The standard deviation measures the fluctuation or volatility of the investment returns. The higher the standard deviation, the more risk you are exposing yourself to. You may make a lot of cash, but you might also lose a lot. However, over the long term, all investments are expected to make you money. Check out the graph below. Notice the clear relationship between risk and return. In order to make more money, you need to take on more risk. That does not mean that putting all your money in one risky tech stock will make you more money though. You should always diversify as the market does not reward the kind of risk that can easily be eliminated through diversification.

	Average Return	Standard Deviation
Small Capitalization Stocks	13%	30%
Large Capitalization Stocks	11%	20%
Fixed Income Securities (i.e. Bonds)	6%	8%
US Treasury Bills	5%	3%

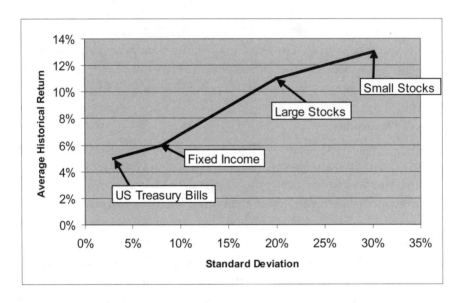

Emotional Investing

We are all emotional beings and although our emotions are often what make us such magnificent people, when it comes to investing they tend to be counterproductive at best. Although our financial goals in life are emotionally driven (retirement, having kids, buying a boat, etc.), the means of accomplishing those goals (investing), has no need for emotions. Instead, common sense, practicality, and, most importantly, self-control are the main ingredients for successful investing. It's investing, not sex, so suppress those emotions and let your brain do the thinking this time.

Fear is the most common emotion confronted in the investment world. Ironically, it seems that fear of losing money often results in the loss of more money than if the fear had never existed. Let me give a few examples.

Example 1: The Stock Market

A very cliché example of investment fear has to do with the stock market. During the market triumph of the late 90s, stock market investors were ecstatic. The market had never seen such a boom. I have an older friend, with substantial investments, who was throwing all his money into the stock market up through 2000. Then the market started to drop and he became weary of its investment potential, so he stopped investing but didn't pull out. He held on until 2002, when the market took another big drop. After that, he said that he could not bear to watch his investments go down any further and he took the majority of his money out of the stock market. He put it into much safer investments and actually held way too much as cash. He was convinced the stock market was a bad investment and was too risky. Sure enough, the market rallied back in 2003. He had very little invested and missed out on large potential profits.

This is a classic example of the "late to the party" phenomenon. In the 90s, this friend saw how far the market had gone up, so he hopped on board, but the market had already gone up. Instead, he was just in time for the market to crash—he was late to the party. Then after the crash, he pulled out, but then the market went up again and he missed out. This friend of mine would have been so much better off if he had simply left his money in the market the whole time. Instead he gave in to his emotions. Most of the more sophisticated investors I know were doing the exact opposite. They had been pulling their money out of the market in the late 90s because the inflated prices were not supported by the individual companies' financial situations. Then as the market dropped, and everyone ran away from the stock market, the sophisticated investors ran to their computers to invest more. These investors used their brains and did not let emotions determine their actions.

Example 2: Real Estate

Another example of emotions ruining people's investments has to do with real estate. In this case though, instead of giving in to fear, they give in to excitement. Real estate has huge profit potential for a number of reasons (see next section). When people discover this they get extremely excited and anxious to invest. I definitely know the feeling, as I felt the same way when I graduated college after focusing my studies and internships on real estate investing. Fortunately, I didn't have quite enough cash to allow myself to make a mistake, as prices were not justified by rents at the time. The numbers just don't always make sense – some real estate purchases are horrible investments. I see too many people who are so excited to buy real estate that they make poor decisions. Similar to the previous stock market example, you typically see this kind of behavior following a large real estate boom. People look around and see how much investors are making and want a piece for themselves, so they scrounge up all the money they can get their hands on and buy some property. If these investors took a moment to calm down and consider the situation, they would realize that it is not sustainable for a real estate market to continue to rise by 20% per year— especially after it had just done so for the past few years. These kinds of investors are also "late to the party".

All of us, of course, have emotions and cannot necessarily rid ourselves of them. In fact, in many parts of life we should welcome them. However, it is very important to learn to control your emotions when it comes to investing. Address their existence and then kick them to the curb, allowing your brain to take over. Emotions can be hard to ignore, but if you give in to them, your investments will pay the price.

Keep Liquid Investments

A liquid investment is one that can be quickly sold without a price discount. For example, money in a savings account is liquid because that money can be immediately withdrawn any time without penalty. Real estate, on the other hand, is illiquid because in order to cash out on a piece of real estate, an investor would either have to sell the property at a significant discount or wait a month or longer for the typical sales process to wind up. Other illiquid assets include trust deeds, certificates of deposit (CDs), traditional IRAs, and antiques.

The world does tend to reward people for taking on illiquid investments. CDs are a textbook example of this—the longer the amount of time you loan the bank your money, the higher an interest rate you are paid. Although increased returns are a rational and justified reason to invest, be careful of how much you allocate towards illiquid investments. Remember the saying that you need to "save for a rainy day?" Well, not only is it important to save for the rainy day, but it's also very important for the money to be accessible when the rainy day comes along. If life throws you a curve ball that requires a chunk of cash and all your money is tied up in illiquid investments, then as my trashy friend would say, you're standing in a pile of horse dung without a shovel. It wouldn't be the end of the world though. You could still withdraw your money; you would just have to pay a hefty penalty. You would be much better off if you have a reasonable amount of money on hand to deal with whatever problems may arise.

The amount you keep liquid depends on your situation and does not necessarily have to be kept in poorly performing safe investments such as a savings account. Some riskier investments, such as the stock market, can also be liquid. If needed, you can often sell some stock and have cash in your hands in a matter of days. Just remember that the stock market is risky and that when you need to access that money, it is possible that only a portion of the original amount will be left in the account. Another way to prepare for financial surprises is to have easy access to other people's money. Depending on your situation, you can establish a line of credit at your bank or, if you're lucky, your parents may be willing and readily able to lend you money as needed. Just don't rely on credit cards to bail you out of financial trouble, as they tend to be better at leading people into financial trouble. Like most issues in personal finance, the way you deal with the liquidity problem depends on your situation and attitude towards risk. The important thing is that you are aware that the future is unpredictable and you have your finances structured in such a way that allows you to efficiently withstand undesired financial surprises.

"Get Rich Quick" Schemes

We've all seen the idiot on late night TV running around with a question-mark suit screaming about how much money the government will give you. And we've probably all been intrigued by the real estate guru's promise to convert us into millionaires overnight if we bought his $350 course. These advertisements have an undeniable appeal, but the results they promise to deliver are far from reality. Think about how the world has to work. There's no way that the world could operate the way it does if any idiot could make a million bucks using some ridiculously simple strategy that he heard on an infomercial. If the scheme was truly that profitable, then why would the creator be selling it on TV? Wouldn't the creator keep it a secret so that he could continue to profit without worrying about competitors? After considering the answers to these sort of questions, you'll discover that "Get Rich Quick" schemes are just plain ridiculous. They rarely pass the common sense test, and therefore feed off people who make emotional impulse purchases rather than logical, fully informed decisions. In the end, all they do is waste your time, steal your money, and let you down.

There are many investment opportunities out there and almost all tend to be portrayed as highly beneficial or profitable. An important aspect to consider when choosing amongst the various opportunities is the method in which you came across it. As a large generalization, investment opportunities that are brought to you in some form or another, perhaps through telephone solicitations, door-to-door salesmen, or late night TV investment gurus, are substandard at best, but often just plain rip-offs. In order to find a truly worthwhile opportunity, you will likely need to seek it out. Good opportunities don't need to be heavily advertised because investors will flock to them. Think about it—does Ben Stiller need to run a classified add that says "actor available for hire"? Of course not. If a movie producer wants to make a stupid, yet totally awesome movie about something like dodgeball or male models, then they will seek him out. The same is true of investments. A truly profitable investment does not need to be heavily marketed or pushed by stock brokers. Why, you ask? Because the profitability of such an investment is evident to investors and profitability sells itself.

Financial Advisors

The financial world can be very complicated at times and, for whatever reason, you may want to seek the advice of a professional. I realize that as a freshly graduated individual with a relatively simple financial situation, the idea of paying a financial planner to help manage your $500 life savings may seem ridiculous, and it probably is. However, if you lack confidence in your financial awareness, you may want to consider at least having one brief consultation with a financial planner. There may be ways to better your situation that you are unaware of and the financial knowledge and habits you develop now will likely pay off tenfold in the future as your investment portfolio grows. If you do choose to seek professional advice, make sure to understand the differences amongst financial advisors, and be selective. Financial advisors can be categorized into two major groups: those who receive commissions in some form or another and those who receive no commissions whatsoever (called fee-only advisors).

Commission-Based Planners

The problem with advisors who receive commissions is that they have an inherent conflict of interest. It is their duty to act in the best interest of their clients, yet they receive commissions based on the financial products they sell their clients. Commission based advisors are inclined to sell the investments that provide themselves with the highest cut instead of selling the investment that best fits the client's needs. To make matters even worse, as a generalization, large commissions are often offered on products that are highly profitable for the seller, which by nature implies that they are a rip-off for the consumer. Commission-based advisors tend to be better salespeople than advisors. On the bright side, advice from commission-based planners is often free or at least cheap.

Fee-Only Planners

Fee-only planners do not receive commissions from brokerage houses or other financial institutions. Instead, they must earn their income solely from the fees they charge their clients. These fees can be collected in various ways. Fee-only planners may charge on an hourly basis, as a flat rate for a specific task (such as preparing a financial plan), as a percentage of the amount you invest, or any mix of these. The main point is that they do not receive commissions. This results in two things: 1) You pay much higher fees and 2) the advice you receive should be unbiased and aimed towards bettering your financial situation and not your planner's.

The Choice

So which planner should you choose? My advice is neither. The best thing you can do to better your financial situation is to learn about it yourself and become your own planner. However, if that is just not your style, then go ahead and see a planner. At first, it may seem that fee-only planners are the way to go. After all, bad advice for free is not a good deal. However, despite the built-in conflict of interest, the advice of a commission-based planner is by no means worthless. As a recent graduate, I would guess that you're not looking to invest $500K so it would be hard to justify paying the high fees charged by fee-only planners. At this age, I would suggest getting advice from a commission-based planner and then check that information on your own before making any decisions.

Chapter 6: What It's All About

There are numerous investment options to choose from. At this point in life, it is best to gather a diverse basket of medium to high-risk investments such as stocks and real estate. With diversification and a long time frame, risky investments can actually be quite safe.

Chapter 7

THE STOCK MARKET

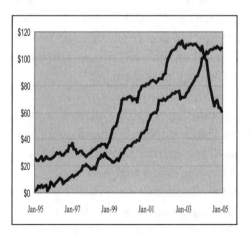

Stocks are a great investment and probably the most appropriate choice for you at this stage in life. Over your lifetime, you will probably invest more in this market than any other. As we saw in the previous section, stocks are risky in the short term, but both profitable and relatively safe in the long run. Since you have a long life ahead of you, long-term stock investing is where it's at. By no means though, should you view the stock market as a short-term investment as its fluctuations are too great and unpredictable in the short term. But how short is short term? For investment purposes, I would consider any money invested for less than five years to be a short-term investment. If you want to buy a new car or house in a few years, do not fully rely on the stock market. But if we're talking about retirement, a future child's education, or simply accumulating more money in the somewhat distant future, then the stock market is the way to go.

Brokerage Accounts

A brokerage account is your primary tool for purchasing investments. It is actually quite similar to a checking or savings account except that money in a brokerage account doesn't have to just sit there—it can be used to purchase many various investments such as stocks, bonds, and mutual funds. Like a bank, many brokerages have local branch offices that you can visit to make deposits and withdrawals. Other brokerages are purely Internet based. With the Internet brokerages, you'll have to make deposits and withdrawals by mail or with electronic transfers from you checking account, which is actually quite convenient.

In order to open a brokerage account, all you need to do is either visit a branch with your initial deposit in hand or follow the steps on the brokerage's website. Once you have your account set up and ready to go, it's time to invest. Keep in mind that each time you purchase or sell an investment, brokers take a commission—that's how they make money. The commission level can vary greatly from broker to broker and also depends on how you trade. By the way, a "trade" is a general term for anytime a stock is purchased or sold. Check out the various stock trading commissions:

Trading commissions typically range from as low as a few dollars up to $25 per trade and much higher if broker assistance is requested. Trading over the internet is always cheaper than trading over the phone. Additionally, some brokers will offer discounted commissions based on the amount you have invested and/or how actively you trade. For example, a popular brokerage firm currently offers $8 trades for customers who have over $500,000 or make 10 or more trades per month, but this same company charges $20 per trade if the customer has less than $50,000 and trades infrequently.

A few considerations:

> *1. How low are the commissions?*
> Brokerages such as Scottrade and Ameritrade are considered discount brokers. They offer very little customer advice or planning services, which allows them to have such low commissions. For someone who just wants to buy and sell investments without receiving broker advice, this is definitely the way to go. At the other end of the spectrum is full-service brokers who offer a comprehensive investment package complete with strategic investment advice and planning. Of course, a premium is paid for this level of service.

> *2. Are Internally Managed Mutual Funds Offered?*
> Some brokers will only facilitate investment trades whereas others may create the investments internally for their clients. For example, companies like Vanguard and Fidelity offer internally managed mutual funds for their clients in addition to providing standard brokerage services. Other brokerages such as Scottrade only offer standard brokerage services.

> *3. Does the Broker Offer Advisory Services?*
> Most discount brokers offer very little in terms of investment advice and planning. They assume you know what you are doing. On the other hand, some premium brokers offer a range of services to their clients. These "full service brokers" charge significantly higher commissions, but can assist clients with practically all financial needs.

Which Broker Should You Choose?

I believe that everybody should have an account with a broker who provides low-cost mutual funds such as Vanguard or Fidelity. But when it comes to purchasing individual stocks and other investments, your broker choice comes down to a single tradeoff: Do you go with a discount broker who gives you little to no advice but has low commissions or do you use a full-service broker that is willing to hold your hand through the investment process but has high commissions? Only you can answer that question, but here's my perspective: it's all about discount brokers. I never use my broker as a source for investment advice and I don't want to hold hands with some old man—that's just weird—so I don't really care which advisory services the company offers. I base my choice of broker purely on fees and commissions. Besides, I would prefer to get my knowledge and advice from an unbiased person who is not going to profit based on my investment decisions.

How Many Accounts Should a Person Have?

Life is complicated enough—there is no point in adding the unnecessary complication of multiple brokerage accounts. Some people collect brokerage accounts like they are going out of style, but for the average investor one or two is probably fine. Even as an active investor, I only have the need for two accounts. I have one with Vanguard, which I use for mutual funds, and one with Scottrade for more active trading.

Market Efficiency

Market efficiency is a common investment concept that plays an extremely important role in stock market investing. However, it also plays a very boring and technical role in stock market investing, so I won't drag you through the theory here. The following statement essentially captures the essence of market efficiency: *A monkey throwing darts at the Wall Street Journal can pick a better portfolio of stocks than a professional stock investor.* The idea is that you are simply indifferent to which stocks you purchase. Because of the thousands of analysts out there, every stock is priced fairly, leaving the market with no good or bad deals. So, on average, any random collection of stocks will perform just as well as a professionally chosen collection. This is only a theory, but because of the compelling arguments in support of it, the rest of this chapter assumes the stock market is mostly, but not entirely, efficient. For a full discussion of the efficient-market theory, read A Random Walk Down Wall Street by Burton G. Malkiel.

How to Invest in an Efficient Stock Market

Index funds. It's all about index funds. An index fund is a type of mutual fund, but rather than heavily researching stocks in an attempt to create the perfect portfolio, an index fund simply mirrors a corresponding index. So if you invest in a large-stock index fund, you are essentially buying a small amount of every large stock in the market. If you invest in a total stock index fund, then you are investing in every stock (large and small) in the market. It's really as simple as that. The benefit of this kind of investing is that it costs less. When mutual fund managers and analysts go out to research potential investments, who do you think pays for all that? You, the investor, of course. But any idiot can manage an index fund—all he has to do is buy a little of everything in the index. Therefore, index fund fees are typically insignificantly small whereas typical mutual fund fees may be substantial.

Choosing an Index Fund

By investing in index funds, you avoid the hassle of researching the numerous mutual funds, but there are also multiple index funds to choose from. So which one do you buy? The most common index fund tracks the 500 largest companies in the United States, but I prefer a less popular fund that tracks the Wilshire 5000 index. This index is essentially composed of the entire U.S. stock market, which of course includes the 500 largest stocks as well as the smaller ones. Historically speaking, smaller stocks have outperformed larger stocks and I would like to get my hands on those larger profits. Large companies such as Google, Microsoft, and General Motors are also much more popular than most of the smaller companies. I tend to shy away from such popular investments because their prices are often unjustifiably inflated.

I would also recommend investing a portion in international index funds. Here you basically have two choices: stable countries (e.g., Europe, Australia, and parts of Asia) or emerging markets (e.g., Brazil, Korea, South Africa, and Taiwan). The stable countries naturally have much lower risk levels and the emerging market funds have substantial risks, which historically at least, have been rewarded with high returns.   If you choose emerging markets, as I have, I can't stress enough how risky they can be. You can lose a considerable amount of money, but of course, you can also make a lot. If you don't mind the risk, just make sure that you don't need the money any time soon and that you invest a relatively small portion of your portfolio in emerging markets.

Below is a summary of the more common index funds available.

Common Index Funds

Large Cap Funds

These funds typically match the S&P 500 index which tracks the 500 largest companies in the United States.

Small-Cap Funds

Only invests in smaller public companies. In theory, small companies are riskier, but also have greater potential profits.

Mid-Cap Funds

As you would guess, these funds invest in all the medium-sized companies. This can provide a nice compromise between risky stocks with high potential profits (small cap) and safe stocks with low potential profits (large cap).

Social Funds

These index funds only invest in those companies that are deemed socially responsible. Naturally, you would not expect to find Smith and Wesson, Playboy, or Philip Morris represented here.

Total Stock Market Funds

These funds typically match the Wilshire 5000 index, which essentially tracks the entire U.S. stock market.

International: Emerging Markets

These index funds invest in extremely risky and unstable economies throughout the world. They have great potential, but also great risks.

International: Developed Markets

The two main funds you'll see here are the European Index Funds and the Pacific Index Funds. Both invest in developed nations similar to the United States and should have similar risk levels.

Bond Funds

The main options here are short term, intermediate term, and long term bond funds. Longer terms mean more risk and higher returns.

Because of globalization of the business world and for the diversification benefits, it is probably a good idea to always include international investments along with domestic. But which funds? All of them can be great investments and your choice should depend on your risk tolerance. So ...

Your Risk Tolerance	Suggested Index Funds
Risk Hater	Large cap domestic funds, international funds in developed markets, and bond funds
Risk Lover	Small cap domestic funds and international funds in emerging markets
Somewhere in Between a Lover and a Hater	Total stock market domestic funds and a combination of international developed and emerging markets funds

The Exception

Up until now, I have implied that the stock market is efficient and everyone should only buy index funds. However, there is an exception to this argument. The stock market has evolved over the years and there have been two prevailing changes: the Internet revolution and the dominance of institutional investing. The majority of stock market investing in today's world is not done by individuals like you and me, but instead by institutions—mutual funds, pension funds, insurance companies, etc. Because these institutions are largely responsible for market efficiency, opportunities can exist in stocks that the institutions overlook. There are two main reasons why a stock may be ignored by the institutions: 1) the company is in trouble or 2) the company is too small to attract institutional interest.

Troubled Companies
When a publicly traded company faces an unfavorable situation, such as possible bankruptcy or a CEO-involved scandal, institutions often steer clear. Their reasoning is partially because many of these situations can result in poor investments, but also because institutions are subject to popular opinion and would be heavily criticized if they owned such taboo investments. Because institutions account for approximately 65% of stock market investing, their disapproval of a particular stock can result in a significant decline in the stock's price. In many situations, the stock is

so troubled that this decline in price is justified. However, there are also situations in which the decline is unjustified and favorable investment opportunities can arise.

A good example of this is with the Northern California-based electric company PG&E. PG&E faced bankruptcy several years ago. There was heavy media coverage and the two main stockholder groups, retired folks and institutions, were afraid to own the stock. This resulted in a large price decline. However, it was clear that the electric company would not be allowed to go bankrupt and so a large decline was not justified. If bankruptcy was to occur, the government would be forced to enter the electricity distribution business, which they were not prepared to do. So what happened? The California government bailed out PG&E and the stock price skyrocketed.

Small Companies

When institutions make investment purchase decisions, they invest a lot of money. It is not feasible to make such large investments in such small companies. On a given day, there are typically few shares of small company stock available for sale and large institutional orders would overwhelm the market. The only way that such large purchases could be made is if the institution paid an inflated price to entice stockholders to sell. Paying an unjustified higher price defeats the point of investing, so institutions tend to just stay clear of small stock.

The beauty of small companies is that the stock market geeks do not analyze them, so it is possible to do your own research and find good deals. An example of this is a stock that I used to own, True Religion. This was a small company (now much larger) with a single product line: high quality denim. I was introduced to the stock by a friend who noticed that the company had a very desirable financial situation and that very few analysts followed the stock. My friend called every True Religion retailer in California and discovered that the jeans had been selling like hot cakes. I asked around in my circle of friends and found similar information. Many of the fashionable girls I knew wanted to buy these ridiculously expensive jeans but could not because the stores were sold out. With all this positive information, it seemed obvious that the company was a steal at its current price, so my friend and I invested. Eventually analysts caught on, company earnings skyrocketed, and the stock quadrupled over a one-year period. If this had been a larger stock that was heavily analyzed, its price would have been much higher because the analysts would have seen what my friend saw. Luckily for us, True Religion was small and ignored, which allowed us to profit.

There can be some amazing deals out there in small or troubled companies, but do keep in mind that there is often a significant amount of risk involved with such investments. The two examples above describe situations in which money was made, but I have also invested in companies in similar situations and lost 50% or more of my investment. The point of this discussion is not necessarily to recommend small or troubled companies as investments, but to simply point out situations in which inefficiencies can arise in an otherwise efficient stock market.

Chapter 7: What It's All About

The stock market should be your primary investment vehicle at this stage in life. Statistics and historical data show that an investor is best off with index funds (i.e., extremely low cost mutual funds) in various sectors of the economy rather than with a standard mutual fund or, even worse, a portfolio of personally selected stocks in the same industry.

Chapter **8**

REAL ESTATE INVESTING

Real Estate Characteristics

Real estate investing can be extremely profitable and exciting. It is a great investment and if done correctly can produce consistent double-digit returns. However, if you're not careful, you could also end up losing everything. From an investment perspective, real estate is attractive when compared to other investments such as stocks and bonds for two reasons: 1) because of the ability to borrow against, or leverage it, and 2) because the real estate market is extremely inefficient.

Leverage
Real estate investment returns have historically been very similar to the stock market – around 10%. So what's all this talk about real estate being such a great investment if you could do just as well by sitting at your computer and clicking the mouse a few times to buy some stock? The reason that real estate can be so profitable is because you can leverage the hell out of it. Leveraging simply means using other people's money. If an investor pays all cash for a piece of real estate, then he is NOT using leverage. But if an investor only puts down a down payment of cash and finances the remaining purchase price with a mortgage, then he is using leverage. In the stock market, an investor can typically borrow only up to 50% of the investment price. But with investment real estate, borrowing up to 80% or more is typical. The increased ability to leverage your investment makes a huge impact on the investment's returns.

Alright, time to get technical. Feel free to skip to the next section, but if you care for a better explanation of leverage, consider the following example:

The Benefits of Leverage	
The Stock Market	**Real Estate**
Unleveraged Return — 10%	Unleveraged Return — 10%
Interest Rate on Loan — 6%	Interest Rate on Loan — 6%
Return from Borrowed $'s — 4%	Return from Borrowed $'s — 4%
Leverage: 50% (for every $1 that you invest, the bank will also invest $1)	**Leverage: 80%** (for every $1 that you invest, the bank will invest $4)
Leveraged Return — 14% (10% plus 4% on each of the bank's $'s)	**Leveraged Return — 26%** (10% plus 4% on each of the bank's $'s)

In previous table, both the stock market and real estate have the same unleveraged return and interest rate. However, as previously noted, the stock market limits leverage to 50% and real estate allows for 80% leverage. So for each dollar you invest in the stock market, the bank will loan you one dollar, but for each dollar you invest in real estate, the bank will loan you four dollars. Each of the bank's dollars will earn a 10% return, but cost you 6%, so in the end each will earn 4%. With real estate, the bank will give you more dollars for each dollar you invest, so your return will be affected that much more. Perhaps a simpler way to look at it: $1,000 invested in the stock market can buy $2,000 worth of stock with leverage, but $1,000 invested in real estate can buy $5,000 worth of real estate with leverage. A $5,000 asset would naturally provide greater income than a $2,000 asset, hence the power of leverage.

At this point you may think that you should borrow as much money as possible for a piece of real estate because it will increase your profit. That's not always true. It is extremely important to note that this magnification of investment profits (e.g. 10% turning into 26% through leverage) works in the reverse as well. Consider the following:

Awesome versus Bad Leverage	
Awesome Real Estate Deal	**Bad Real Estate Deal**
Unleveraged Return 8% Interest Rate on Loan 5% Return from Borrowed $'s 3%	Unleveraged Return 8% Interest Rate on Loan 10% Return from Borrowed $'s -2%
Leverage: 80% (for every $1 that you invest, the bank will have $4 invested)	**Leverage: 80%** (for every $1 that you invest, the bank will have $4 invested)
Leveraged Return 20% (8% on your $'s plus 3% on each of the bank's $'s)	**Leveraged Return** 0% (8% on your $'s minus 2% on each of the bank's $'s)

These two real estate deals are almost identical except for one important aspect—the awesome deal has an interest rate that is lower than the unleveraged return whereas the bad deal has an interest rate that is higher than the unleveraged return. So with the bad deal, each dollar borrowed from the bank earns 8% but costs 10%. The more you borrow, the more you lose. In such situations, leveraging real estate through debt can be disastrous. To sum it up, leverage magnifies investment returns. It makes the good times great and the bad times terrible. Many investors are entirely unaware of this relationship and learn the hard way.

Market Inefficiencies: Heterogeneity

As we previously discussed, the stock market is relatively efficient—it is hard to earn excess profits because the stock prices are constantly analyzed by professionals and therefore current prices are representative of current economic values. This is not true of the real estate market, where amazing deals are more common. There are multiple factors that contribute to market inefficiency, but perhaps the most important is that every property is unique in its own way. Because of design, quality, size, and particularly location differentials, no two pieces of real estate are identical, making generalization and accurate analysis difficult. You can undoubtedly state that today's price for a share of Microsoft is $27.19, but there's no way that you could state that a 2,500-square-foot 4-bedroom home is worth $500,000. This may be close to true in Sacramento, California, but the exact same home might cost $140,000 in Montana or $1.8 million in the Florida Keys. Even within the same city, prices of otherwise identical homes can vary drastically based on proximity to city resources, the surrounding atmosphere, construction quality, and many other external influences.

Market Inefficiencies: Geographical Fixity

Another key characteristic of real estate is that the investment is geographically fixed. I can buy a hundred shares of stock in Krispy Kreme Donuts from my California home, then sell it to an investor in New York who can turn around and sell it to an investor in Japan. A share of stock has no geographical fixation. Real estate, on the other hand, is primarily a local market. It doesn't make much sense to buy distant property, mostly because you likely know very little about distant markets and therefore increase the odds of making poor investments, but also because it is very difficult to manage out-of-town property. As my old real estate finance professor put it: "I won't invest in real estate that I can't walk to." The fact that most real estate markets are localized also implies that they have a smaller number of buyers and sellers than if they were nationalized or globalized like the stock market. With fewer buyers and sellers, there is less competition and the possibility of finding "good deals" increases.

Market Inefficiencies: High Transaction Costs

Besides having homogeneous investments with no geographical fixation, another prerequisite of an efficient market is the ability to make transactions quickly and efficiently with little or no transaction costs. Again, real estate defies this requirement. Selling property can take months or even years and often results in large transaction costs (e.g., broker fees, lost rental income, escrow fees, etc.). In order to dispose of a piece of real estate quickly, a significantly discounted sales price is typically necessary. This may be an undesirable attribute for those who want to sell real estate ASAP, but it can also be a tremendous opportunity for investors who are readily willing and able to purchase real estate. You don't see these sorts of opportunities in an efficient marketplace. For example, I can sit down at the computer and immediately sell any stock that I own at market price for a very minimal brokerage fee (around $10 with most discount brokerages). So no matter how desperate I am to sell my stock, nobody can take advantage of my desperation by ripping me off. In real estate markets, when people need to sell property fast, they are often forced to accept a substantial price discount in exchange for a quick, effortless sale. For an opportunistic real estate investor, this is an ideal situation.

Other Characteristics

Real estate investing can be very exciting and profitable, yet also relatively complicated. It is also important to note that having a large chunk of cash for a down payment is typically a prerequisite. This combination of complexity and large investment size has a tendency to scare potential investors away from the real estate market. The investment process can also be confusing at times; even with a stable property that you've owned for years, headaches are not uncommon. You cannot simply sit back and check on your property a few years later to see how it's doing the way you can with many other investments. Real estate investing requires attention and regular maintenance.

Although the preceding characteristics are all undesirable, it is because of their existence that real estate has so much profit potential. The market rewards investors for taking on such burdens. Think about it: Why would anyone tie up such a large amount of money for such a long time period and deal with all the other hassles involved with real estate, unless they were going to be rewarded with higher profits?

Investment Strategies

Now that you realize the potential and have a little background on the real estate market, let's look at some investment strategies. Similar to all investments, the two main investment strategies for real estate are "buy and hold" (long term) and "flipping" (short term). The buy and hold strategy is what we generally think of in regards to real estate investing. You simply buy a property, maybe hire a property manager, and sit back while income from rent flows in and you pray for high appreciation. At the other end of the spectrum you have "flipping," which is buying a property and then quickly selling, or flipping, it for a higher price.

Regardless of the strategy, the most important part of any real estate deal is the purchase. You make or lose money when you buy, not when you sell. This is the one main factor that you have control over. You can't force somebody to pay you a certain level of rent each month and you can't force a buyer to pay you X amount of dollars when you eventually sell the property. However, you can set the price you are willing to pay. The seller may not agree with your price and you may not acquire the property, but that's OK. This is preferable to overpaying and being locked down to a bad deal. Like I said, the money is made when you buy. Once the purchase is made, the deal is set up. You will collect a predictable amount of rent and have a predictable amount of expenses. Then some months or years later you will sell the property for an unpredictable price, which is completely out of your control. Sure you can fix up the home and market it like crazy, but if you overpaid in the first place, these efforts may have a minimal effect on profit. Again, money is made upon the purchase, not the sale, which explains why most real estate investment strategies focus on getting good deals rather than how to sell for a high price.

So how do you get the good deals? Basically, just determine what a property is worth and then offer the owner a lower price. If it is accepted, then awesome—you got a good deal. If it is not accepted, then no big deal, you just move on to the next house. It's basically a numbers game: Make a ton of lowball offers and eventually one will work out.

Determining Value

You're probably thinking to yourself "Yeah, that sounds good, make a ton of lowball offers and wait for someone to bite. But how low of an offer? How the heck do you know exactly what a piece of real estate is worth?" Well, good questions. You can't really place an exact value on any piece of real estate for many reasons that I won't go into, but what you can do is determine a ballpark value that a person would reasonably pay for the house. The way I do this is by simply asking a real estate broker in the area to get me some comps. The term "comp" stands for comparable and is used in the real estate industry to describe a recently sold home that is similar to the property being analyzed. For example, let's say that I am looking to buy a three-bedroom, two-bath house in San Jose, CA. I would simply walk into a broker's office and tell an agent that I'm considering the purchase of a home in the area and was hoping she could provide me with some comps for a three-bedroom, two-bath home. I would give her the address, or at least the general location, the square footage, and any other pertinent data. She will provide a list of recently sold properties, which will include all important information such as sales price, square footage, and a property description.

Pick out the properties that are most similar to the home you want to purchase and adjust for any differences such as a swimming pool, superior condition, landscaping, etc., to arrive at an estimated value. This is essentially the process used by real estate appraisers, although they are much more thorough and provide unnecessarily long reports full of useless information along with their value estimates. If you want to get into real estate investing, understand this process. I have barely touched on it here, but you should know that value estimation is arguably the most important tool that a real estate investor can possess and is the key to successful fundamental investing.

Getting Greedy

So now that you have estimated the value for a certain property, how much do you offer? How low do you go? This depends. You want to get the lowest price possible but you also want the deal to go through. If there are other offers on the table and yours is too low, then the seller will reject yours and go with the higher offer. On the other hand, you don't want to overpay.

The only advice I can really give you is to not get greedy. When I first began looking at real estate as an investment I was in college. I didn't have nearly enough money for a down payment, but figured if I found a good deal I could get the money from other investors. I recall trying to buy single-family homes at a substantial discount, offering a price $100,000 below market value. Of course, I was unsuccessful. Eventually, I got the speech from my father: "Daniel, I'm proud of your ambition", he said, "but you're never going to make money doing this. You're looking for a steal. What you need to be looking for is a deal, and there are plenty of those around." He brought up a great point. Steals don't come around very often—maybe a few during a lifetime. However, deals are plentiful and a person with less greed can make many deals that, over time, can result in significant wealth. You are much better off making deals. I'm still a big fan of lowballing, as long as it's not ridiculous. Ideally, you want to make an offer slightly below what you think the seller would agree to, but not so low that the seller will completely reject the offer without making a counteroffer.

When to Invest

Whatever investment strategy you are using, timing is an extremely important consideration. Let's start off by looking at the flipping strategy. Think about what's going on here. You are purchasing a property at a discount and immediately turning around and selling it. It is preferable to do this kind of investing in a seller's market, when there are more buyers than sellers and, because of the high demand, real estate sells quickly. While flipping a piece of real estate, the property is typically vacant. Therefore, you lose a lot of money each month the property does not sell. Even worse, if too much time goes by, property values may decline and you may incur substantial losses.

Now let's consider the more typical buy and hold strategy for long-term investing. What's going on here is fairly straightforward. You purchase a house, you collect rents, then sometime down the road you sell for a higher price. With this strategy, timing is everything. I'm not going to pretend that I can predict when real estate prices will change and in which direction they will go in the future. Sorry, my dog ate my crystal ball. The real estate market is such a complicated mix of ever-changing emotions and logic that it's almost impossible to accurately predict price changes. However, we can still determine with relative accuracy when it makes sense to invest.

We may not be able to predict the future, but we do have data on where the market has been and we can also analyze the present. Don't focus on how much higher or lower the market will go because who knows when it will decide to change directions. Instead, ask yourself this question: "Does this piece of real estate make sense today, the way it is, regardless of future appreciation?" Let the answer to that question guide your decision on when to invest. When I consider a real estate purchase, I focus primarily on cash flow. In other words, I only like real estate investments in which the rental income is at least enough to cover my expenses (mortgage, property taxes, insurance, repairs, etc.). Then, regardless of future appreciation levels, my investment will do fine. This may sound obvious, but you would be surprised how many people purchase real estate relying only on appreciation. This kind of investing is extremely risky because appreciation is such an unknown variable.

In certain parts of the country, particularly places like Florida and California, where property values have recently run through the roof, investors are currently purchasing real estate with very negative cash flows. In many cases, they are losing something like $500 every month. This may seem crazy, and I would agree, it is. The reality of the situation is that these investments are very emotion driven. In the past few years, real estate in California has skyrocketed. Everyone who lives there has witnessed prices rise and then rise some more. Those who got in early are doing quite well. Those who did not get in early have watched those who did become wealthy. Now, they are jealous and want a piece of the action. This is a horrible situation. Not only are they buying into a negative cash flow investment, but they are also late to the party. The market has already gone up. They missed it. It might go up a little more, who knows, but it's already unjustifiably high and eventually it must correct itself. Prices may fall, but the more likely scenario is that they will simply stay flat for a while (i.e., have 0% appreciation). It's actually quite ironic. This is arguably one of the worst times to buy, yet it is also the time that investors are the most excited and optimistic about real estate. This sort of irrational decision making is often accompanied by investing based on appreciation speculation. On the other hand, investing based on cash flow is rather predictable—you know the expenses you will incur and you can easily determine the rental revenue by looking at the surrounding rental market. This way, any appreciation is just a bonus rather than your sole source of profit.

However, using cash flow alone as criteria for real estate investing is not sufficient. Appreciation potential should at least be considered. Cash flow still comes first, but you will want to invest in a desirable location that has the potential for appreciation. For example, in a college town, a property near campus is clearly more desirable and has greater appreciation potential than the house on the outskirts of town next to the railroad tracks. The two properties may have similar cash flows, but the house near campus has a better location and therefore has higher appreciation potential. This does not necessarily mean that it will appreciate more than the other property, but it does have more going for it and if one of the houses were to rise in value, I would put my money on the one near campus. Also, consider what would happen if the local market changed and there was an oversupply of rental real estate. The property next to campus would still bring in cash flow, but the property next to the tracks would likely be vacant.

The Poor Man's Guide to Real Estate Investing

You may have seen the moron on late night TV pushing a certain no-money-down investment course. He preaches the concept of making millions of dollars in real estate without using any of your own money. Schemes such as this are to be avoided, although I have to admit that when I was younger and very anxious to start investing, I was a sucker and called in to buy a similar program. My dad warned me, but I bought it anyway and learned the lesson firsthand.

There is, however, a bit of truth to the no-money-down concept. The catch is that in reality, a profitable no-money-down deal is quite difficult to come by. Nonetheless, it is definitely possible for the ambitious and energetic soul. The following are a few of the more realistic options for the broke real estate investor. But keep in mind that each of these is extremely challenging and often risky.

Option 1: Second and Third Mortgages

In the recent past, many banking institutions issued second and third mortgages for up to 100% financing of real estate purchases. First mortgages are typically for up to around 80% of the purchase price. The bank may then lend you up to 20% more through a second and possibly third mortgage. You are probably wondering why the banks don't simply issue one big mortgage instead of three. There is a good reason. The first 80% loan is a relatively safe investment for the bank. If your home goes down in value and the bank has to foreclose because you failed to make the mortgage payment, it is likely that at least 80% of the original value is still there. However, when the bank loans 95 or 100% of the purchase price, then the loan is much more vulnerable to real estate price declines. Therefore, banks create second and third mortgages as separate loans with much higher interest rates. This form of 100% financing has been widespread in the recent past, but its presence may fade in the near future. Banks will lend money to anybody with a pulse these days, but it's only a matter of time before interest rates rise and the real estate craze comes to a close. Then, housing prices will stabilize, people with variable rate mortgages will default on their loans, and banking institutions will become much more conservative with their lending practices and limit, if not eliminate, 100% financing deals—at least that's my prediction.

Option 2: Seller Financing

While negotiating with the owner of the house, ask if he or she is willing to provide some level of seller financing in the form of a second mortgage. The bank would provide you with somewhere around 80% of the purchase price and the remaining 20% would be paid back to the seller through a second mortgage. Unlike the typical mortgage from a commercial bank in which the loan is paid back over a 30-year term, seller-financed mortgages typically specify a 5, 10, or maybe 15-year payback period. A 30-year term is possible but unlikely because most sellers want to be paid back sooner than later. The interest rate will have to be negotiated. You should shoot for a rate similar to that of your first mortgage, but a little higher should be acceptable.

Of course, in order to structure such a deal, the seller needs to have a lot of equity in the property. How much equity the seller has can easily be obtained by asking the seller or by looking through the county records on the property. To access county records, you can either go to the county recorder's office or simply ask a realtor or title company employee.

Option 3: OPM (Other People's Money)

We have all heard the saying "it takes money to make money." But who ever said that this money had to belong to you? My former finance professor used to tell me: "There are far more people with money in this world than there are truly good investment deals." This is a simple point, but also one of the best lessons he ever taught me. If you can find a truly good deal, investors will beg you to let them in on it. But how do you find these investors? Friends or family perhaps, but in the interest of maintaining distinctive personal and business lives, unrelated individuals from a local investment club may be a better option. Such clubs can be easily found through the Internet. Once you have investors, you would then write up an agreement that specifies how the profits are to be split. Keep in mind that if you are putting up little to no money, you will likely be expected to put forth the most effort in the deal.

Option 4: Flip the Contract

The term "flip" is real estate slang for purchasing a property and immediately selling it for profit. Flipping the contract is essentially the same thing as flipping the property except that you never actually take ownership of or pay for the property. Here's how such a deal would go down: Besides the obvious information, your offer should include two important provisions. First, you should try to get the longest escrow period possible; the longer the time between the offer acceptance and the closing of the deal, the more time you will have to flip the contract. The other thing that your offer must contain is a contingency, or a way out of the deal. A common example is to say that "This offer is contingent upon my partner's approval." This is actually a very general statement and for all the seller knows, your "partner" could be your cocker spaniel back home. This general statement can get you out of almost any contract. Now, assuming the offer is accepted, it is time to find a buyer. Keep in mind that you are not selling the house, only the contract to buy the house. In order to sell the contract, you may want to advertise in the classifieds, talk with realtors, or make an announcement at a local investment club meeting. If the property is under contract for a high price, it is unlikely that you will be able to find a buyer, so it is important that you find a good deal to begin with.

Real Estate Investment Trusts (REIT's)

Real estate is a great investment with high returns. However, because of the large down payment needed and the complexity of the transaction, you may find it undesirable at this stage in your life. Luckily, there is an alternative, hassle-free way to invest in real estate, even when cash is limited.

A REIT, which stands for Real Estate Investment Trust, is essentially a mutual fund of real estate. There are many different REITs out there and each has its own focus. Some REITs buy only property in a certain city, others buy only certain property types such as large apartment complexes or public storage units or residential real estate. Investing in one of these REITs, say, a residential REIT, creates a much more diversified real estate portfolio than simply buying a single home because your investment is spread out amongst many different properties. Nonetheless, you still have all your money in a single real estate sector, and could therefore benefit from further diversification. Perhaps the best option is to invest in a REIT index fund. Many investment brokers offer REITs, but I have seen relatively few REIT index funds. I know that Vanguard offers one and that there is also an exchange traded fund, which you can buy with any brokerage account, with the ticker symbol RWR. With a REIT index fund, you can allocate your money amongst many different REITs, giving you a truly diversified real estate portfolio.

The historical average returns on REITs are actually quite similar to those of the stock market. During a recent 30-year period, REIT returns averaged 14.18%, while U.S. stocks averaged 14.82%. Although the long-run returns are similar to the stock market, the real estate market's ups and downs have little correlation with the stock market's ups and downs, which provides important diversification benefits.

Chapter 8: What It's All About

Because of its unique nature and the fact that every investment is different, real estate can be extremely attractive with huge profits. However, it also requires a lot of cash and can be a headache. If you take on too much investment debt you might obtain excessive profits, but you are also more susceptible to bankruptcy. Real estate investing is definitely not rocket science and it does make millionaires out of many people, but first-time investors should be extra cautious. It is easy to find good real estate deals, but it's just as easy to find horrible ones.

Chapter **9**

INSURANCE

The purpose of insurance is to provide protection from unexpected financial problems. Do not ignore it. Insurance is probably the least exciting topic in personal finance, but it is extremely important as well. There are many financial problems that can occur in life, ranging from your $40 eBay purchase being damaged in the mail to someone suing you for $2 million because he slipped and fell on your driveway. Insurance is offered on most financial threats, including these two, so the question is: What type of insurance should you buy? As a general rule, I recommend buying insurance only in situations in which you are unable to handle the potential loss. As for the previous two examples, I don't think many of us have $2 million to lose, but I would hope that we could all make ends meet after losing $40 in the mail. I realize that you don't want to lose the $40 and that you would have been better off by simply paying $2.10 for eBay insurance in order to save the $40 purchase. But that view is too narrow; you need to consider the overall picture, including the insurance company's point of view.

Insurance companies are businesses and, like all businesses, they exist in order to make a profit. On average, they need to take in more money than they pay out, so on average you should expect to receive something like 90 cents back for every dollar you spend on insurance. Not only do your insurance premiums go towards the insurance company's profit, but they also pay for employee salaries, marketing costs, and company overhead, such as rent and supplies. The odds are not in your favor. You would be much better off by taking a one-time $40 hit than spending $2.10 thirty times in order to save $40 that one time your eBay purchase is lost or damaged. On the other hand, depending on your situation, you might not be able to afford to bear the risk of some potential tragedies such as crashing your car, being sued, needing extensive surgery, or losing your home to a fire. In situations where the loss would seriously affect your financial well-being, insurance is a good idea. But if you can easily afford to bear the risk of the loss, then do not purchase insurance for it. The following is a brief overview of the more common types of insurance available:

Auto Insurance

Bodily Injury Liability

Bodily injury liability insurance compensates the passengers in your car as well as those in the other car for an accident in which you are at fault. It is quoted as two numbers (i.e. $50,000/$100,000). This quote means that in an accident, the insurance company will pay up to $50,000 per person, but no more than a total of $100,000 per accident. For example, if you purchased $50,000/$100,000 and had an accident in which three people were injured, each with $40,000 in medical bills for a total of $120,000, your insurance company would pay only $100,000. Alternatively, if the accident results in only one person being injured with $70,000 in medical bills, your insurance company will pay only up to the "per person maximum," or $50,000. Every driver is required by law to have this insurance, but how much coverage you buy is up to you. Wealthier people may desire $100,000/$300,000 coverage, but something around $50,000/$100,000 should be sufficient for a young person earning under $40,000 per year who doesn't own a home or any other substantial assets. Think about it. Would you hire security guards to protect a vacant warehouse? Probably not, so why hire an insurance company to protect non-existent assets? That's just my opinion though. You will need to make your own decision.

Property Damage Liability

This insurance covers physical damage to the property of others from an accident in which you are at fault. It is required by law, but you can choose how much coverage you buy. Similar to bodily injury liability insurance, it doesn't make sense to buy a lot of coverage here if you don't have assets to protect. A $50,000 policy should be sufficient, but if it helps you sleep at night, go with the $100,000 policy.

Collision

Collision insurance pays money to the automobile owner for damage to the owner's car in situations in which the owner caused the damage. So if I crash into a light pole or rear-end somebody and damage my car, then collision covers this damage. If the accident is somebody else's fault, then that person's liability insurance will cover my damage. Unlike auto liability insurance, collision insurance is completely optional. Whether or not you should purchase it and what deductible you choose are questions that only you can answer. For financially secure individuals who are confident in their defensive driving abilities, collision insurance might be an unreasonable purchase. However, if you cannot afford to pay for auto repairs and/or you see yourself as an accident-prone driver, then purchasing collision insurance may be quite justified. If you do choose to purchase collision insurance, it's usually a good idea to get the largest deductible as this will decrease your premium substantially.

Comprehensive

Comprehensive auto insurance covers damage to your vehicle resulting from things other than a collision. This includes things such as trees falling on your car, gravel from the freeway cracking your windshield, or some punk kid throwing a pumpkin through your back window on Halloween. If you choose this option, an insurance inspector will check out your car and take note of the current condition before granting you coverage, so don't bother trying to get comprehensive insurance after the car has been damaged. Generally speaking, comprehensive insurance is another one of those small and relatively expensive types of insurance that you may be better off without.

Uninsured Motorist

This kind of insurance will pay for you and your family's medical bills in case of an accident with an uninsured driver or a hit and run. It is relatively cheap ($40 or so a year for $100,000 worth of coverage) and is probably worth purchasing.

Health Insurance

Your health is not something you want to take chances on. Everybody should have some level of health insurance. Typically, health insurance is included in the benefits package you receive from your employer. If it is not included or you are self-employed, you need to purchase an individual plan.

HMO or PPO

There are two primary forms of health insurance plans. The first is a Health Maintenance Organization (HMO). Under an HMO plan, you are limited to using a specified network of doctors. Doctor visits outside of the network are not covered by the insurance company. The advantage of an HMO is that it is relatively inexpensive. The disadvantage is that you have little choice of physicians. The other form is a Preferred Provider Organization plan, or PPO plan. A PPO allows for much more flexibility in physician choice. Of course, this flexibility will cost you. Neither plan is necessarily a better deal. Your choice will depend on your lifestyle and preferences.

Coverage

Once you decide on the type of plan you desire, you need to choose your level of coverage. There are many considerations here, including:

Co-pay: This is the amount that you pay every time you visit the doctor. Between $5 and $50 is typical.

Professional Services: This would include services such as lab tests and x-rays. The insurance company will typically pay a specified percentage of these expenses and you will pay the remaining amount.

Hospital Services: Coverage here is typically the same as Professional Services coverage.

Annual Deductible: You will have to pay everything up to the annual deductible before insurance will pay you a single dime. After the deductible is reached, costs are split according to your plan. Doctor visits are typically the exception; the insurance company will cover these costs (less your co-pay) regardless of your deductible.

Prescription Drugs: The typical options are no coverage, generic brand only coverage, and comprehensive coverage. I have chosen generic brand coverage as there is typically little to no difference in brands when it comes to prescriptions.

Premium: This is the amount that you pay for the insurance, typically on a monthly basis.

How much coverage you should purchase is up to you. Just make sure that your decision corresponds with your needs. You do not want to compromise your health in order to save a few bucks. As a healthy, young adult who rarely sees the doctor, I have chosen high deductibles, high co-pays, yet low monthly premiums. I am basically only insuring for major medical problems.

Preexisting Conditions

Your monthly premium will obviously depend on your level of coverage but also on any preexisting medical conditions. Anything in your medical records that implies poor health can increase your monthly premium. If the condition arises after you purchased insurance, then you're in the clear. However, if the condition existed beforehand and it was documented somewhere in your medical records, then you must report it. It is tempting to hide such conditions from the insurance company, but that could be troublesome. If you lie on your insurance application and the insurance company discovers this, they can decline any claim or sue you for the amount of claims already paid. This is not worth risking, so make sure to report any preexisting conditions.

And don't be too worried about reporting certain health problems. Especially if they've been resolved, they're not that big of a deal. If insurance companies denied coverage to everyone with any health issues, then they would be out of business. I recently purchased individual health coverage and reported two sport-related injuries, a concussion, and a stomach ulcer. My application was still accepted and the premium was not increased.

COBRA

Don't worry about what COBRA stands for—just know that it refers to the law that allows people to maintain their health insurance for up to 18 months after leaving a job. Your employer will no longer pay the premiums, but at least you can stay insured. The reason COBRA is important to you is because it also applies to college students. You are allowed to remain covered by your parents' or the university's health plan for up to 18 months after graduation. It is important to always have health insurance and COBRA is a great way to maintain coverage while looking for a job, traveling, or just being a bum.

Vision

Vision insurance is a joke. It's a perfect example of the kind of insurance that you would be better off without. The premium you pay usually gets you only one or two eye exams and a new pair of glasses each year—after a deductible of course. This is something you can probably afford yourself. Remember that the insurance company is a business and plans on profiting from you, so if you can afford to bear the loss, such as paying for a pair of spectacles, then it is best not to purchase the insurance.

Dental

Dental insurance is similar to vision. It often covers such small and predictable expenses, that it may not be worth purchasing. For young, healthy individuals who clean their teeth regularly, it often makes sense to simply save money for the biannual teeth cleaning and have a little savings set aside for the occasional filling.

Homeowner's Insurance

There are three main components to a homeowner's insurance policy: structure, personal property, and liability coverage. There are several kinds of policies that differ based on which perils you would like covered. Your choice depends on your personal living situation. For example, if you live in Florida, you may not be concerned with damage due to frozen pipes and so it does not make sense to insure against that peril. Once you have chosen the appropriate policy, you need to determine your coverage.

Your home's market value has two main components: the value of the structure and the value of the land. One must consider that the land often accounts for a large portion of the property's value and, unless a meteor hits your home, the land and its value will be preserved. Therefore, you should only consider the structure's replacement cost for homeowner's insurance purposes. Replacement cost estimates can be obtained on a dollar per square foot basis from most major homebuilders in your area. But should you insure for the entire replacement value or only a fraction of it? Consider the worst-case scenario, which is probably a fire. In most urban or suburban neighborhoods, it is extremely unlikely for a structure to completely burn to the ground. There is almost always a significant portion of the home remaining, so it does not make sense to insure against the loss of the entire home. However, insurance companies have written their policies with reparations for clients who insure for less than 80% of the structure's replacement cost. They allow you to do this, but then require you to pay a portion of every claim, even those within the coverage limits. Therefore, the rule of thumb when it comes to homeowner's insurance is that a home should be insured for exactly 80% of its replacement cost.

The second component of homeowner's insurance covers your belongings inside your home. The amount of coverage you should obtain depends on the value of your belongings. You may want to walk around your home with a video camera to inventory everything you own to avoid any discrepancies regarding an insurance claim. To obtain the lowest premium, it is a good idea to buy the policy with the highest deductible.

The last part of a homeowner's policy is liability coverage. As with auto liability insurance, the amount of coverage you purchase here depends on the value of your assets. There's no rule of thumb here – how much to buy is mostly a personal decision based on the person's risk tolerance.

Renter's Insurance

Renter's insurance and homeowner's insurance provide the same coverage except that renter's insurance does not insure the actual building. As a renter, there's no reason for you to insure the home because you don't own it. Your landlord will take out a policy to insure the building, but it is up to you to protect yourself against liability lawsuits and damage to your belongings. Whether or not you purchase renter's insurance should depend on the value of your assets. When I graduated college, half of my belongings were held together with duct tape and I had little money in the bank. I had nothing to protect and was not about to buy renter's insurance. However, if you have been working for a while, have substantial savings, and own valuable furniture and home electronics, then it may be a good idea to purchase renter's insurance.

Umbrella Insurance

Umbrella insurance is a general liability policy that typically covers you for large amounts of money above and beyond what your other policies pay. For example, if you are sued for $1 million and your homeowner's policy covers only $300,000, then the umbrella policy will step up and pay the remaining $700,000. Because an umbrella policy provides coverage only if a claim is in excess of the standard policy, it is rarely called upon. It is therefore relatively cheap and worth purchasing if you have substantial assets to protect. But as a recent graduate, I wouldn't worry about it for now. It would be silly to purchase a $3 million umbrella policy when your only asset is a rusty old '96 Honda Civic.

Life Insurance

For most recent graduates, life insurance just doesn't make sense. It does serve an important role in society, which is to provide financial help to those who have lost their breadwinners and cannot sufficiently support themselves (e.g., a disabled woman whose salary-earning husband died in a car accident). It also makes a lot of sense for families with financially dependent children. What would happen if you were to pass on? How would your children afford to live, eat, and go to school? However, unless you got a head start in life, I assume these are not your current concerns. If you don't have anyone who depends on you, there is no need for life insurance. Besides, buying life insurance is basically placing a bet on

> Death Benefit: The amount of money that your children or other beneficiaries will receive upon your death.

yourself to die, and that is just plain creepy. If you decide that you do want life insurance for whatever reason, just make sure to purchase term life insurance, not whole life insurance. For the same death benefit, whole insurance costs more, but it combines the death benefit with a savings plan that you can cash out at any time. However, the savings plan provides very poor returns and you would be much better off buying term life insurance and setting aside the difference (which you saved by not buying whole insurance) in some sort of investment account. You will have the same death benefit either way, but under this method your savings will be much higher than if you used the savings plan under whole life insurance. Unless you have horrible spending habits and no discipline when it comes to saving and investing, there is absolutely no reason to buy whole life insurance. If you didn't follow that, no worries, just don't buy life insurance unless you have dependents and even then do not buy whole life insurance.

Disability Insurance

If you become disabled (knock on wood!), this form of insurance will provide you with a stable income until you are able to return to work or, in the case of permanent disability, for a specified time period. If you're married and your spouse earns sufficient income, then it may be unnecessary. But for those of us who are single or are the primary breadwinners in the marriage, then purchasing at least partial disability coverage may be a smart decision.

Mail Insurance

I loathe this form of insurance. Yes, sometimes things do get lost in the mail, but it doesn't happen all that often and paying $2 in order to insure a $30 eBay purchase is just plain silly. I've probably purchased around 50 items on eBay averaging $30 each and have yet to have one lost or damaged in the mail. If I had purchased insurance for each, I would be out $100. Even in the unlikely event that my next three $30 purchases are lost, I'm still better off without the insurance. EBay is profiting from people's fear of losing their small purchases. Insuring a computer or other expensive good is one thing, but don't insure your $15 DVD (even if it is the unrated version of Deuce Bigalow European Gigolo).

Computer Service and Support

Yes, this is a form of insurance. The only difference from the other forms above is that your claims are settled with advice and support instead of with cash. Think about a few things when deciding whether to purchase service and support. First off, you, or maybe a good friend, might be tech savvy enough to troubleshoot most problems, and therefore it might not make sense to buy service and support. Or maybe your computer use will be limited, so the likeliness of problems arising is slim. On the other hand, if you plan on using your computer often for a variety of tasks, problems will be inevitable and it might make sense to pay for service and support. Also, keep in mind that since claims are not settled in cash, purchasing this form of insurance is not necessarily a statistically bad bet, unlike most other types of insurance. The cost to the computer company for providing you support is likely far less than you would have to pay a third party to assist you. If it costs them $50 to help you, but you would have to pay $150 otherwise and the service and support costs $100, then everyone's happy and so it is possible for both you and the computer company to benefit from this sort of insurance. Personally, I am an incompetent idiot when it comes to computer viruses and troubleshooting, so I always pay for service and support.

Shopping Around

Once you have decided to purchase a certain form of insurance, don't just drive to the closest insurance company and sign up. Insurance premiums can vary significantly amongst brokers, so make sure to shop around. There are four main methods of obtaining insurance. There are brokers who represent a single insurance company, independent brokers who represent several companies, direct marketers who sell policies through the Internet or 1-800 numbers, and group policies obtained through an employer. No generalization can be made regarding the best option, just make sure to shop around and compare premiums in order to find the best deal.

Just as you would shop around when you initially purchase insurance, do the same every year or two when it comes time to renew your policy. Similar to cell phone plans and credit card deals, insurance companies may offer promotional deals to new clients in order to attract business. Check out other companies; if a better deal exists, inform your insurance company. If it won't beat the deal, switch companies.

Chapter 9: What It's All About

The purpose of insurance is to protect yourself from financial disasters only, not every single potential loss. If you can afford the loss in question, there is no reason to insure against it. Some forms of insurance, such as health and auto liability, are essential, but small insurances such as vision and dental should be avoided when possible.

Chapter **10**

TAXES

Now that you've graduated, your parents no longer file your taxes for you and your life will slowly become more and more financially complicated. You will soon develop a severe hatred for the IRS. April 15th will become a day of depression on which you lock yourself in a room filled with tax forms and, while trying to get your computer in a scorpion death-lock because it told you that you owe the IRS money, you contemplate escaping to the Mexican border in order to avoid writing such a large check. Okay, so it's not quite that bad, but still, taxes suck. They are obviously extremely necessary (unless you believe in anarchy), but that doesn't mean that we can't still bitch about them. On the bright side, there are ways to minimize the amount we pay Uncle Sam. But first, a little overview of the tax system.

The Tax Process

Filing

Not everyone has to file. If you are single and had income less than $8,200, then you do not have to file taxes. However, if you had a job in which money was withheld from your paycheck, then it is in your interest to file, because you are almost guaranteed a refund. So how do you go about filing? As a starting point, you should get three things:

1. *Publication 17* – This is the general book regarding income taxes. It will hold your hand through the entire process.

2. *1040 Tax Form* – This is the main form that takes you through the entire process. All other forms are supplements and flow into the 1040. If your tax situation is simple, this may be the only form you need.

3. *1040 Instructions Manual* – This booklet is a must and will guide you through the 1040 form step by step.

These resources are free of cost and are all published by the IRS. They can usually be picked up at your local post office or library. Also, assuming your state levies an income tax as well, make sure to pick up any state income tax forms and instructions while you're there. All forms, instructions, and publications are also available at www.irs.gov along with many other resources. Chances are that as you go through the 1040 form, you will discover you need other forms or schedules, which you can always print from the IRS website.

How Taxes Are Calculated

Gross Income
– Adjustments
Adjusted Gross Income
– Deductions and Exemptions
Taxable Income
× tax rate(s)
Total Tax
– Credits
– Withholdings
Tax Bill or Tax Refund

Gross Income

Unfortunately, this amount is not limited to your salary. The IRS also demands you report any income from tips, stock dividends, interest, profit from asset sales, alimony, rental real estate, and basically anything else that placed money in your pocket. As for asset sales (e.g., stock sales), only those that you owned for less than one-year are taxed as income. Investments that you held for over one year are taxed at the lower capital gains tax rate (currently 15%). This is definitely something to consider when you are selling investments. Sometimes waiting that extra week or so to make a sale can make a huge difference on your tax bill, so keep that in mind.

Adjustments

Adjustments have the same effect as deductions (see below) except that they are allowed regardless of whether you itemize deductions or take the standard deduction. Adjustments include such things as moving expenses, educator expenses, tuition, traditional IRA contributions, and student loan interest. The amount spent on these categories is subtracted from your gross income and decreases the amount of tax you pay.

Deductions: Standard or Itemized

You have two options when it comes to deductions: You can either take the standard deduction or you can itemize deductions. Whichever option results in the largest deduction is of course the option you should choose. The standard deduction is a flat amount that you are allowed to deduct from your income. It is currently $5,000 but usually increases each tax year. Itemizing deductions means that you can deduct your actual expenses as long as they fall within certain IRS-defined categories. These categories include various expenses such as taxes paid, interest payments, gifts to charity, and job-related expenditures. As a general rule, you will probably just take the standard deduction until you own your own home. The interest component of mortgage payments is usually huge in the first few years of homeownership and this amount should easily exceed the standard deduction.

Because job-related expenses fall under itemized deductions, certain careers can also lend themselves to itemizing deductions. For example, my first job out of college was in real estate appraisal. I basically spent every day driving around the state. Employees are currently allowed to deduct $0.485 for every job-related mile driven (not including the commute to and from work), so a real estate appraiser will almost always itemize deductions rather than taking the standard.

Exemptions

For each dependent, you are allowed to deduct $3,200 from your income in the form of an exemption. It's called an exemption, but don't let this confuse you—it has the exact same effect as a deduction. Unless your parents still claim you as a dependent, you are allowed to take an exemption for yourself. So, just to clarify, a typical recent grad who has $35,000 in income and is not claimed as a dependent by her parents is allowed to subtract the $5,000 standard deduction as well as a $3,200 exemption from her income, leaving her with a taxable income of $26,800.

Tax Rates

Our federal tax system is based on a progressive tax. What this means is that as a person earns more and more money, a larger portion of her income goes to taxes. Compare this to a flat tax, where everyone pays the same percentage of their income in taxes. The table below is taken from Publication 17 and applies only to those filing as single—there are different tables for married couples. The numbers in this table will change each year.

If your taxable income is:		The tax is:	Of the amount over:
Over:	But not over:		
$0	$7,300	---------- 10%	$0
$7,300	$29,700	$730 + 15%	$7,300
$29,700	$71,950	4,090 + 25%	$29,700
$71,950	$150,150	14,652 + 28%	$71,950
$150,150	$326,450	36,548 + 33%	$150,150
$326,450	-----------	94,727 + 35%	$326,450

Let's go through a quick example for a person with a taxable income of say...$35,000. The first $7,300 would be taxed at 10%, which amounts to $730. The amount from $7,300 to $29,700 would be taxed at 15%, which amounts to $3,360. The amount from $29,700 to $35,000 would be taxed at 25%, which amounts to $1,325. All together the total tax owed would be $730 + $3,360 + $1,325 = $5,415.

Credits vs. Deductions

There are two general ways to decrease your tax bill: credits and deductions. Deductions are explained above and include things such as interest payments, donations, and employee expenses. Almost everyone has at least a few expenses that fall into this category. The only question is: Are these expenses greater than the standard deduction? Credits, on the other hand, are not quite as common. A tax credit can be rewarded for certain situations such as paying for your own education, being disabled, or having little income while raising children. The main difference between deductions and credits is that given the same dollar amount of deductions or credits, you would much prefer a credit. Here's why: A deduction is subtracted from your income and then your tax rate is applied to the remainder. Credits, on the other hand, are applied to the amount of tax you owe. So deductions are taken before tax and credits after tax. Assuming a 30% marginal tax bracket, a $1,000 deduction would decrease your tax bill by $300 whereas a $1,000 tax credit would decrease your tax bill by $1,000.

Withholdings

When you receive your paycheck, money is typically withheld and applied towards income taxes. As much as we hate having money taken out of our paychecks, there is a good reason for this. If the IRS did not withhold anything, then come April 15th when taxes are due, you would likely have a fat bill that you might not be prepared to pay. The IRS is not accustomed to forgiving its debts, so failure to pay taxes will likely result in significant credit problems and possibly criminal charges. So in a sense, you might want to be thankful that the IRS withholds money from your paycheck. Me? I'm more spiteful than thankful.

Do Your Own Taxes

Taxes are by far the largest single expense we incur over our lifetime (unless you haven't worked a day in your life and sleep in gutters). Therefore, you should learn as much as possible regarding your specific tax situation. There are many ways to reduce taxes and it's important that you are aware of the various strategies. Sure you can pay a professional to do them for you, but consider the sacrifices. First off, professional tax accountants often charge a hefty fee, which you would prefer to avoid. Also, being fresh out of college, your tax situation is likely quite simple. Without dependents, real estate, alimony, a private business, or other complicating factors, doing your own taxes is well within your capabilities. Although it's great to avoid the expense of paying a professional, that is perhaps the least significant argument for doing your own taxes. The important thing is that by doing them yourself you can really learn the process and therefore gain valuable insight into how life choices affect your tax bill and how you can maximize deductions. You may think that a professional would be best at maximizing deductions, but that's not always true. Sure, they could be better, but they often choose not to in order to protect their practice. Questionable deductions can result in an audit and after a number of audits, a tax accountant's reputation could really be hurt. You can't blame professionals for being cautious, but it can be a conflict of interest if they avoid deductions that you want to take. You should never lie about your income or make up deductions, but the tax code has a lot of gray areas. If you believe certain deductions to be valid, you may want to take them. As long as you're not making stuff up, you can simply view tax forms as an opening negotiation with the IRS. The tax forms say how much you are willing to pay and if the IRS doesn't agree, then it can audit you and you can discuss a fair solution. The IRS knows how complicated tax law can be and understands that mistakes are made. Usually, the worst the IRS does is simply force you to retract any questionable deductions and recalculate your tax bill. However, if you do completely make up deductions or hide income, you may be subject to tax fraud law. That's a bad thing, so don't lie on your taxes. If you are found to be fraudulent, not only are you subject to being charged with a crime, but your odds of being audited in future years will grow astronomically because you are placed on the IRS's "red flag" list.

Tax Computer Programs

Computer programs such as TurboTax and TaxCut make it easy to do your taxes. Rather than entering the same information many times on all the different forms and researching through thousands of pages of tax code, you simply answer a series of questions and the forms are filled out for you. It's hard to argue against such convenience, but I'm going to try. Here's the problem: By using computer programs to do your taxes, you are learning little about the tax code. By filling the forms out yourself and reading through the instructions, you will gain an understanding of the tax process and be better able to plan for and minimize future taxes. Do yourself a favor and avoid computer programs for the first year or two while your tax situation is simple. From then on, you might as well use computer

---

Chapter 10: What It's All About

Do your taxes yourself and understand the laws that apply to your specific situation. There is so much focus on earning money yet tax minimization is largely neglected. You will pay more money in taxes than anything else in your life, so a little knowledge is worth acquiring.

Chapter **11**

SAVING FOR RETIREMENT

Think it's crazy to start planning for retirement when you're so young? Well, it is, but it's also smart. Social security is being phased out and you cannot count on anyone but yourself to provide for your retirement, but that's beside the point. The real issue is that taking advantage of IRAs and allowing your cash to grow tax free results in too much investment growth to pass up. The government does not want to pay for your retirement, and therefore offers huge incentives in the form of tax-free accounts to individuals who take care of their own retirement.

The Power of Compound Interest

If the Native Americans had taken the $24 worth of trinkets and beads they received for the sale of Manhattan Island in 1626, sold them all, and then invested the $24 at 8%, today that investment would be worth $112 trillion!! With that amount Native Americans could not only buy back Manhattan Island today but probably a few other metropolises as well. That is the extraordinary power of compound interest. Take this power and apply it to your life by starting to save now. Don't wait until you are 30 or 40 to start saving. Developing disciplined savings principals at a young age is extremely beneficial and is a great step towards obtaining significant future wealth and financial independence. It really cannot be emphasized enough. If you take away anything at all from reading this book, let it be this simple lesson. I could blab on and on here, but perhaps the best way to show the importance of saving and investing early in life is to simply let the numbers do the talking. Check it out:

Started Saving at age 40	
Monthly Savings Contribution:	$400
Invested at:	10%
Amount Accumulated by age 60:	**$303,748**

Started Saving at age 20	
Monthly Savings Contribution:	$400
Invested at:	10%
Amount Accumulated by age 60:	**$2,529,632**

This is a huge difference! Although the investment's time period only doubled, the savings accumulation over a 40-year time span is eight times the amount accumulated over a 20-year time span. Every dollar you save today is much more significant (in fact, as we just saw, roughly eight times as significant) than each dollar you save 20 years from now. By understanding and applying this power, all young people have the potential to accumulate great wealth or at the least provide themselves with a comfortable future living. It just takes a little discipline.

The Beauty of Tax Free Growth

There are two different kinds of IRAs: Roth and traditional. With a traditional IRA, the amount you contribute is tax deductible, so you avoid paying taxes on that money when it is earned, and instead pay taxes on it in the future when you retire and make withdrawals. A Roth IRA is the opposite. A contribution to a Roth IRA is not tax deductible. Instead, you pay taxes on that money when it is earned and no taxes are due upon retirement.

Either way, you are required to pay taxes. The beauty of it is that you pay taxes only once and the investment is allowed to grow tax free. Under normal non-IRA circumstances, taxes are levied on initial earnings, and then again on the investment growth. Perhaps an example will better explain.

Mary is 25 years old and is looking to put some cash into the stock market, which yields an estimated 11% return. The table below shows the growth of a one-time contribution to a stock market investment account under non-IRA circumstances. Keep in mind that Mary pays taxes when she initially earns the money and then again as the money grows. If she invested in the stock market, there would be two tax rates: the marginal tax rate and the capital gains tax rate. For simplicity sake, let's assume she invests in the bond market with an 8% annual return and no capital gains. Here's what would happen:

Non-IRA Account	
Marginal Tax Rate	35%
Amount Invested	$4,000
Annual Return	8.0%
After Tax Rate of Return	5.2%
Amount After 30 Years	**$18,303**

The after-tax rate of return above is simply the full 8% return multiplied by 65%. The reason for this is that you may be earning 8% on your investment, but 35% of that is taken by the IRS, leaving you with 65% of your return, or 5.2%. Now take a look at the growth of an identical investment under a Roth IRA in which the investment grows tax free.

IRA Account	
Marginal Tax Rate	35%
Amount Invested	$4,000
Annual Return	8.0%
After Tax Rate of Return	8.0%
Amount After 30 Years	**$40,251**

Roth or Traditional?

When approaching this question, a logical person might think to themselves: "OK, with a Roth IRA, I pay taxes now and with a traditional IRA, I pay taxes later. So if I anticipate my tax rate upon retirement to be lower than it is currently, I should go with a traditional IRA, but if I anticipate my tax rate upon retirement to be higher than it is currently, than I should go with a Roth IRA." But how the heck do you know what tax rates will be in 35 years? Here's my advice: Show your middle finger to the traditional IRA and then go open a Roth IRA.

Here's why. First off, guessing what your tax rate will be 35 years from now is a crapshoot. Life is very dynamic—who knows what your income and tax rates will look like by then. Secondly, a Roth IRA allows you to access your money as described in the following sections. And most importantly, a Roth IRA allows you to invest more pre-tax dollars.

You are currently allowed to invest $4,000 in either a traditional or Roth IRA. But that $4,000 is actually 4,000 pre-tax dollars (i.e. no tax was paid on this money) for the traditional and 4,000 after-tax dollars (i.e. tax was already paid on this money) for the Roth. If we convert the Roth's 4,000 after-tax dollars to pre-tax dollars, then assuming a 35% tax rate, the Roth actually allows you to invest 6,150 pre-tax dollars. This results in higher potential profits, so I recommend Roth IRAs. See the table below if you care for further explanation.

Traditional vs. Roth IRA		
Marginal Tax Rate	30%	
Rate of Return on Investment	8%	
	Traditional	*Roth*
Maximum Contribution	$4,000	$4,000
Initial Tax Savings (placed in Non-IRA Account)*	$1,200	$0
IRA Balance after 30 Years	$40,251	$40,251
Non-IRA Account Balance after 30 Years	$6,153	$0
Total Investment Balance	$46,404	$40,251
Less: Taxes due on IRA Distributions	($12,075)	$0
Total Amount Available (after tax)	$34,329	$40,251
* Due to the fact that a traditional IRA is tax deductible - we assume this money is placed in a normal taxable account.		

The Catch

There is an obvious and large benefit to IRA investing, but of course there is a catch. First off, the investment is limited to a certain amount per year. The maximum contribution is currently $4,000. In 2008 this amount will be increased to $5,000. But the real catch is that you cannot touch the money in an IRA until you reach the age of 59 ½ unless you are willing to not only pay income tax on the distributions but also a 10% penalty. You can move the money around to other investments, but you cannot make a withdrawal and go shopping. However, there are a few key exceptions to this "hands off" policy.

Exceptions to the "Hands Off" Policy

Many young adults hesitate to invest in an IRA because, first off, who in their right mind is worrying about retirement right now? More importantly, they don't invest because they want to have access to that money in case something comes up. Well, luckily, with a Roth IRA, you can withdraw up to the amount you contributed free of income tax and the 10% penalty. So if you invested $6,000 in a Roth IRA account several years ago and now it is worth $7,500, then you can withdraw $6,000 without paying taxes or the 10% penalty. However, if you take out any amount in excess of $6,000 (which would be considered profit), then that excess will be taxed and subject to the 10% penalty. Another important exception is that the government allows you to withdraw up to $10,000 (regardless if the money is contributions or investment growth) tax and penalty free as long as it is used to purchase a first home. This is significant, since buying a first home is often the most important reason we would need access to our money at this age. Because of these wonderful exceptions, there is almost no reason not to invest in a Roth IRA.

401k and 403b Plans

Most 9 to 5 jobs offer some sort of benefits package. A typical component of these packages is a 401k or, if you work for certain non-profit institutions, a 403b plan. These plans are simply tax-deferred investment accounts. Money is deducted from each paycheck and added to an account where it grows free of taxes. You can contribute up to $15,000 for the 2006 tax year subject to any limits established by your employer. Of course, you don't have to contribute anything if you prefer not to. As far as tax treatment goes, the 401k and 403b are taxed essentially the same as a traditional IRA. The main difference is that 401k and 403b plans are set up through the employer and an IRA is set up by the individual. You are allowed to make contributions to both. Another benefit of 401k and 403b plans is that employers will often match a certain level of your contributions. That's right—every dollar that you put in, your employer will put in the same amount up to a specified limit. No offense, but if you don't take advantage of this, you're an idiot. It is essentially free money—an immediate 100%

return on your investment. Check with your employer about their plan though. Employer matching is quite common, but does vary from employer to employer. Some don't offer it, some will only match every dollar you invest with $0.25, and some will match every dollar you invest with one, two, or even three dollars! However, many employers will not allow you to contribute to the plan until you meet certain requirements such as working for at least six months. If your employer does match contributions, by all means contribute. And if you don't ... slap yourself.

Chapter 11: What It's All About

Contribute as much money as possible to retirement accounts. The benefit of tax-free growth is quite impressive. By the time you retire, an amount invested in a tax-free account can result in more than double the profit than an equivalent amount invested in a taxable account. And with a Roth IRA, your money can still be accessible prior to retirement.

Chapter **12**

HOME, SWEET HOME

Renting

As you will see in the following section, buying a home can provide tremendous savings over the years. However, it is usually not an option during the first few years following college. Therefore, you likely have two options: You can move back in with the folks to save money, which would be a great financial move, but trust me, a horrible social move—a wild night out consists of running into your only high school friend who is still in town at a Blockbuster and watching a movie with her folks—or you can of course lease a house or an apartment by yourself or with some buddies. As you probably know from the college years, this option tends to be a lot more exciting and, despite the increased cost, I definitely recommend doing so if you can afford it. Assuming you have chosen to lease a house, here are some tips that may be useful.

Negotiating Rent

Yes, it is quite possible to obtain a lower rent than is advertised. Of course, the amount of a discount, if any, that you can receive is highly dependent on the current market situation. If limited rentals are available and there are many potential tenants, then there is little chance to negotiate rent. However, in a market with an oversupply of rentals, you have a lot of negotiating power and should definitely at least ask for a rent discount. As with any negotiation, take a minute to consider the situation. Think about what you want out of the deal and, most importantly, put yourself in your opponent's shoes to consider his desires and his fears. A landlord typically has two main fears that you can easily take advantage of. Vacancy is by far the worst of the two. If a landlord is not collecting rent, then the house or apartment is just a sinkhole that he throws money into. Each month the property is vacant, the landlord is missing out on a lot of potential money and is often willing to accept a lower rent. Think about it: If you were a landlord, would you rather rent your place out for $800/month now or keep it vacant for a few months in order to obtain $900/month? A few months of vacancy can be a huge loss to the landlord. The other fear that landlords typically have is disrespectful and destructive tenants who have trouble paying rent. You would be amazed at what some tenants do to a home. My parents once had a tenant who tore down the entire backyard fence for firewood!

When negotiating with your landlord, it is important for him to like you. Dress appropriately, look clean cut, and, regardless of whether or not it is true, give the impression that you will not throw parties, play loud music, or burn the fence in the fireplace. Basically just try to act like the perfect tenant. References from prior landlords, a credit check, and maybe proof of employment, such as a paycheck, will also help relieve any concerns that the landlord may have. As for the discount, don't ask for too much—50% off is just not going to happen. However, a discount of around $100 each month would be quite reasonable. You may have to try several landlords, but finding that discount will be well worth the effort. Keep in mind that everything is negotiable. Other things you may want to bring up with the landlord are the day of the month rent is due, how much money is required for the security deposit, and what services (water, garbage, DSL, etc.) the landlord will be responsible for.

The Walkthrough

Make sure to take note of any damage to the property and point it out to the landlord. Many landlords will have a walkthrough sheet on which you note all damage and then both sign. If the landlord does not provide one, it is a good idea for you to make one up yourself. Don't worry about making it professional—I think I used binder paper and a colored pencil for the one I made. It doesn't take long and it could save you from wrongful damage charges at the expiration of your lease.

The Lease

Read it all the way through and make sure you understand each section. I know it's a contract, which is short for "boring crap that you don't want to read," but in this case it is important crap since it determines your living situation for at least the next several months. Most of the time the lease will be acceptable, but you never know what rules a landlord may try to impose upon a tenant, so play it safe and make sure to read it all. Most importantly, make sure that any roommates you have sign the lease as well. Trust me, as you've probably learned in college, many things can go wrong with otherwise good roommates. If your roommates are not on the lease, they have no legal financial obligation. They could damage the house or take off without paying rent and, as far as the landlord is concerned, you signed the lease, so you are responsible.

Homeownership

Purchasing a house for yourself is arguably the best financial move you could make at your age. The benefits that you will reap through homeownership are huge. Not only will you essentially fix your housing costs as your friends continue to pay higher and higher rents, but you will also gain equity in your home as it appreciates. Therefore, saving your hard-earned cash towards a down payment might be the best financial move you could make right now. See the renting versus purchasing comparison below to see how homeownership could benefit you.

Notice that during the first year, the rental amount is only slightly lower than the cost of ownership. However, looking at year 7 and beyond, the cost of ownership becomes much less than the cost of renting. The reason for this is simple yet important. Rent generally increases at a rate similar to inflation (3% in our example) while the largest expense of owning a home, the mortgage payment, is fixed and does not increase at all. Also, keep in mind that this example completely ignores appreciation, which is one of the most important benefits to owning a home. If we were to account for appreciation as well, the difference would be ridiculously large and in favor of homeownership.

Year	Mortgage Payment	Other Ownership Expenses	Total Ownership Expenses	Annual Rent
1	19,959	4,900	24,859	21,600
2	19,959	5,047	25,006	22,248
3	19,959	5,198	25,157	22,915
4	19,959	5,354	25,313	23,603
5	19,959	5,515	25,474	24,311
6	19,959	5,680	25,640	25,040
7	19,959	5,851	**25,810**	**25,792**
8	19,959	6,026	25,985	26,565
9	19,959	6,207	26,166	27,362
10	19,959	6,393	26,352	28,183
11	19,959	6,585	26,544	29,029
12	19,959	6,783	26,742	29,899
13	19,959	6,986	26,945	30,796
14	19,959	7,196	27,155	31,720
15	19,959	7,412	27,371	32,672
16	19,959	7,634	27,593	33,652
17	19,959	7,863	27,822	34,662
18	19,959	8,099	28,058	35,702
19	19,959	8,342	28,301	36,773
20	19,959	8,592	28,551	37,876
21	19,959	8,850	28,809	39,012
22	19,959	9,115	29,075	40,182
23	19,959	9,389	29,348	41,388
24	19,959	9,671	29,630	42,629
25	19,959	9,961	29,920	43,908

General Assumptions	
Price of home	$ 300,000
Loan Amount	$ 250,000
Monthly Mortgage Payment	$1,663
(30-year, 7% loan)	
Monthly Rent	$ 1,800
Inflation	3%

Annual Ownership Expenses	
Property Insurance	$ 600
Property Taxes	$ 2,300
Water, Sewer, Garbage	$ 500
Maintenance	$ 1,500

Although, the numbers above illustrate undeniable advantages to homeownership, it is important that you consider your situation before diving into this large financial commitment. When I graduated college, I knew the benefits of owning a home and had a strong desire to do so. However, I didn't know where I was going to be five years, two years, or even six months from that time. With so much uncertainty, it just didn't make sense to buy a home. And with such high real estate transaction costs, it is counterproductive to own a home for such a short time period. It is likely that the first few years after graduation will be filled with uncertainty, but as soon as you begin to settle down, I would urge you to consider purchasing a home.

Getting a Home Loan

So you've been eating out of garbage cans and stealing quarters out of fountains for the past few years in order to save up a down payment for a house and you finally have enough. Great job! It is time to purchase that house. But wait, you only have a down payment. Now you need a mortgage. Getting a home loan is not as easy as it sounds. There is a process, which can be confusing and annoying. In order to ease this process and obtain the lowest interest rate, you will want to understand the lender's perspective. Some of the more important factors that lenders take into consideration are outlined below.

Establishing Credit

In order to establish credit, all you need to do is use it. The reason for establishing credit is so that you can receive a low interest rate when it comes time to make those big purchases such as a first home. Mortgage brokers are very hesitant to loan money to a young person who has no credit history, so establishing credit should be a priority if you have not done so already. However, you don't need to use a lot of credit in order to establish credit. It is a big misunderstanding that the more credit you have, the better your credit history and score. In fact, it can often be the opposite. Between one and three sources of credit should be sufficient. Student loans, credit cards, installment loans, and car loans all count towards your credit. Mortgage brokers want to know that you have the discipline to make monthly debt payments but they don't want customers who over leverage themselves with 10 credit cards, a car loan, and a big-screen TV loan from Best Buy. So much credit can be worrisome for lenders, lowering your chances of obtaining a competitive mortgage rate.

A mortgage broker friend of mine recently told me that lenders usually like to see a few credit trades established for at least one year, but if you have enough income to back up your loan they don't really care if you have established credit or not. So what does this mean for you? If credit has been nonexistent in your life and you would like to borrow money eventually, it is probably a good idea to at least get a credit card. However, if you already have at least one credit card, it seems unnecessary to throw away money on interest for a car or TV loan for the sole purpose of establishing credit. It particularly makes little sense when you consider the fact that your income level is the primary determinant for home loan approval.

Keep in mind that the establishment of a credit history can be a good thing, but only if it is a good history. A bad credit history is actually much worse than no credit history. The quality of a person's credit is measured with a FICO score.

FICO Score

Think of this as a credit responsibility score. Its purpose is to place an objective value on the quality of your credit history in order to help lenders make informed credit decisions. A FICO score typically ranges from 350 to 850. Exactly how these numbers are calculated is top-secret, classified information—probably hidden in Area 51 with the aliens and President Bush's SAT score. However, we do know certain things that will lower a FICO score—we just don't know by how much. Try to avoid the following as they have been known to result in a lower score:

> ➢ Making payments after the due date (the later they are, the more it affects your score).

> ➢ Having too much credit.

> ➢ Allowing your credit to be pulled too often (this occurs essentially every time you apply for any sort of credit).

> ➤ Claiming bankruptcy. Don't get into this situation – it's credit suicide. A bankruptcy can stay on your credit report for up to 10 years. Any credit that you are granted after claiming bankruptcy will almost always be for a low amount with an unusually high interest rate.

The purpose of the FICO score is primarily to help lenders decide whether or not they will grant you credit as well as what interest rate and fees will correspond to that loan. I recently called a major banking institution and received quotes for a $300,000 home loan for two consumers who are identical in all respects except for their credit scores. Here is what I found:

Borrower	FICO Score	Interest Rate	Points ($'s)	Additional Fees	Monthly Payment
Mr. Smart	700	6.0%	$0	Minimal	$1,799
Mr. Dumbutt	550	7.5%	$7,500	Lots	$2,098

As you can see, there is a huge difference in the two loans. Check it out— Mr. Dumbutt would pay 2.5 points, or $7,500, plus additional fees, plus an extra $300 per month in payments for the duration of the loan. That sucks! Just remember, it's up to you which of these two borrowers you will be. Use credit responsibly and pay your bills on time and you will be rewarded.

Loan to Value Ratio (LTV)

Just like the name implies, this is the amount you are borrowing divided by the price of the house you are purchasing. For example, a $400,000 home with a $300,000 loan has a 75% LTV. So, the smaller the loan, the smaller the LTV. Lenders prefer a lower LTV for obvious reasons. Your home is their collateral in case you default on the loan. But homes values rise and fall as the market changes, so the lender's collateral will also rise and fall with the market. In the previous example, the value of the $400,000 home could fall by up to $100,000 and the loan would still be sufficiently secured. However, what if the LTV was 100%? In this case, any decrease in home values would result in a risky situation for the lender. Now if the borrower defaults on the loan, the lender would get a house worth less than the mortgage, so the lender would lose money. As a general rule, the lower the LTV (which implies a larger down payment), the lower your interest rate will be.

Income

This is perhaps the most important factor. Lenders want to make sure that you have the ability to make your monthly mortgage payments. Even if they have plenty of collateral because of a low LTV, there is no point for them to make a loan that is just going to go into default. It's a waste of their time. Lenders use what is called an affordability ratio, which is basically your total amount of monthly debt payments divided by your monthly gross income. Each lending institution has a threshold level (usually around 33% to 40%, but up to 55%), above which they won't lend. So if you make $60,000 per year, or $5,000 per month, and the lender uses a 40% affordability ratio, you can allocate $2,000 per month to debt. Use a financial calculator or online mortgage calculator like the one at www.mortgage-calc.com/mortgage/simple.php to find out how much of a loan this corresponds to. Assuming a 6%, 30-year, fully amortized loan, you could borrow $335,000. But don't forget that any existing monthly debt payments will get deducted from that $2,000, resulting in a significant decrease in the amount that you can borrow for a home. (See page 57).

Shopping for Rates

You would think that rates would be the same across the board from bank to bank, but this is not true. Call different banks and ask the current rate for customers in your situation. Give them the information outlined above (your FICO score, the LTV, your income, and any other debt payments you currently have) and they should be able to get you a quote. Make sure to also ask how much the closing costs are and if there are any points on the loan. Remember, you're only inquiring here. Do not actually apply for a loan with all these lenders, as that will result in your credit being pulled many times, which will lower your credit score. Only apply with the lender whom you decide upon.

The Internet is also a great resource for home loans. Check with low cost Internet banks such as www.INGdirect.com as well as websites such as www.bankrate.com, which searches hundreds of lenders for the lowest rates. Of course, your rate will depend on your income, FICO score, and LTV, but the advertised rates can be a good starting point.

Points

A point is basically an upfront fee of 1%. So if you are getting a $300,000 loan and the lender charges 2 points, you will have to pay a $6,000 upfront fee on top of any closing costs. Points are usually thrown in with the mortgage, so you get $300,000 towards your home purchase but your monthly payments are increased in order to pay off the entire $306,000. Don't take points lightly—they represent a huge cost of the loan. People can be fooled into paying them for two reasons. First, as was just explained, you don't actually see the large payment go from your pocket to the lender because it is included with the mortgage and you pay it off slowly with your monthly payments. Second, borrowers who pay points are often enticed by lower interest rates. If a lender is getting $6,000 in points, they can afford to lower the interest rate slightly.

This issue represents a dilemma: How much of a decrease in interest rate is worth paying a point? Assuming you keep the loan for the entire 30 years, a 0.1% or greater decrease in the interest rate is worth paying one point. However, few people actually hold loans for this long. Generally, if you plan on keeping the loan for only a few years, then the decrease in interest rate is likely not worth paying the extra point(s). On the other hand, if you hold the loan for at least 10 years, then the benefit of the decreased interest rate will likely outweigh the cost of the point(s). Personally, I avoid points because they just complicate the situation and I never really know how long I'll want to keep a loan. Interest rates may fall and I'll want to refinance or maybe I'll want to sell the property for whatever reason. I figure that, more often than not, the decreased interest rate is not worth the points I would pay.

Brokers

All a broker really does is shop for a loan. In exchange for this service, brokers tack on fees to the loan, which can be thousands of dollars. If you are confident doing your own shopping, then you have no need for a broker.

Low-Income Housing Programs

Low-income housing programs are common in many cities and can offer huge benefits for the first-time homebuyer. Check with your city for available programs and find out if you qualify. Each city or county will have its own unique program, but here are a few I have come across.

> ➤ The city gives you a loan for $120,000 to be used towards the purchase of a first home. The rate is extremely low at only 3% simple interest and you don't have to make any payments until you sell the home. At that point, you will have to pay back the full $120,000 loan plus interest.

> ➤ A home in a new development is sold at a significant discount from market price. For example, a $325,000 home is sold to a low-income qualifying family for $250,000. The home cannot be sold for full market value until a certain number of years have gone by. If you hold the home for the minimum time period established by the city, you can reap huge profits. Otherwise, you have to resell the home at a discount to another low-income qualifying family.

> ➤ Similar to the above program, a home from a new development is sold to a low-income individual at a significant discount. However, in this case, the portion that was discounted becomes the city's share in the home. The buyer still owns and has full rights to the house, but when it is sold, the city takes back its proportional share.

> ➤ If you are only looking to rent, there are also low-income options. Many apartment complexes are required to offer a certain number of units to low-income families or individuals at substantial discounts.

Two main components are common with low income housing programs. The first is an income ceiling. In order to qualify for any of the programs you must have an income below the ceiling. The amount of income that is considered to be low will be different for every city, but somewhere between

$20,000 and $40,000 is typical. The other main component is a minimum holding period. A certain number of years usually must go by before the home can be sold for market value. If you think you may qualify, it is definitely worth the time to check out what your city has to offer.

Save 6% on Buying a Home

Every time a home is sold, a commission is paid to the real estate brokers involved in the transaction. The standard commission is 6% (3% to the listing broker and 3% to the buying broker). A typical home in Davis, California where I went to college is around $600,000 right now. Saving 6% on that purchase would equate to $36,000, which is a good chunk of cash. The only way to accomplish this is to buy a home that is not currently listed with a real estate broker. In order to find a potential seller who does not already have a realtor, you will have to play the numbers game. Send out tons of letters to homeowners asking if they would be interested in selling their property. Don't worry about any details such as the offer price for now. As you would expect, most people are either not interested in selling their property or they have already listed it with a broker, so you will hear back from only a small fraction of the people you solicit. Here's a tip to try to increase the number of responses: Only send letters to non-owner-occupied homes. Most people would sell their rental house well before their own beloved home. But how do you know if a house is a rental? In college towns, it is often obvious. If there are five junkie cars, seven bicycles, and a bunch of red plastic cups scattered across the front yard, then the house is probably a rental. However, in most cities, it's not always that easy. One method is to visit all the property management companies in the area and obtain rental listings. Another option is to ask a title company for a list of all homes that have the tax bill sent to a different address, which implies a rental. After you mail out all your letters, you just have to wait.

If you hear back from anyone interested in selling, then it is time to evaluate the property and negotiate with the owner. You could hire an appraiser or decide on an offer price yourself based on a list of similar properties in the area that recently sold, often referred to as "comps" (for comparables). Comps can be easily obtained from most real estate agents or title companies. Keep in mind that your estimated price should be based on a standard sale, which includes the 6% broker commissions. Explain that fact to the owner and make an offer for 94% of the estimated price. Because you were the one to seek out the seller and organize the transaction, you should be able to make an effective argument for the 6% decrease. If you can successfully organize this kind of deal, you will save tons of money. But keep in mind that it often requires a good deal of effort and you must be relatively knowledgeable regarding the real estate transaction process.

Save 2% on Selling Your Home

Most recent graduates have yet to purchase their first home, so I realize that a tip regarding the sale of a home is likely of little use to you. Nonetheless, this easy-to-use tip can provide great savings in the future when you do sell a home, so keep it in the back of your head until that time.

Assuming you plan to sell the home in the traditional manner (i.e., with a listing broker), you will be charged a 6% commission. However, like most parts of life, that is negotiable. When you walk into the broker's office, sit down with an agent to discuss the sale of your property. After all the small talk and the basics of the sale are laid out, inform the agent that you will only be paying 4% commissions on the sale. Odds are that she'll refuse to do it for anything less than 6% because that is the policy. Then you say something along the lines of "I understand, but unfortunately I too have a policy where I only pay 4% commissions. I'll try the broker across the street." Give the agent a business card and tell them to give you a call if their policy changes. There is a good chance that it will miraculously change to "4% commissions are acceptable." When you sit back down to discuss the sale, give the agent another surprise by telling her that the 4% commission is to be split 3% to the buyer's agent and 1% to her, the listing agent. There will probably be some huffing and puffing, but she should agree to this split. There is good reason for splitting commissions in this manner. First off, listing brokers have very little work to be done. All they really do is put the property on the MLS (multiple listing system) for all other brokers to see. They may also hold an open house, but that is irrelevant. In reality, open homes are a tool for realtors to meet prospective clients. They don't sell homes.

Under no circumstances should the buyer's agent be assigned less than 3% of the sales price. The reason for this is simple: If an agent is showing a prospective buyer all the houses in the neighborhood and most homes allocate 3% of the sales price to the buyer's broker but your house allocates only 2%, then guess which house is going to be the last stop on the home tour? That's right—yours. And you would be lucky if it was even a stop at all.

There are other less conventional methods of selling property that allow similar savings. For example, you can completely eliminate real estate brokers and list your home for sale in the newspaper, which theoretically would save you 6% of the sales price. However, because your home would not get as much exposure to potential buyers, you would likely be forced to sell for a lower price. Companies such as Help-U-Sell are other options. For a relatively small fee, they will place your property on the MLS, but the rest is up to you. There are multiple alternatives to paying 6% commissions and, with a little effort, lower commissions can be achieved.

Chapter 12: What It's All About

As soon as you settle down in a certain region, purchase a home ASAP. On top of the tremendous sense of pride and accomplishment inherent in homeownership, purchasing your first home will likely make a superior investment. Make sure to consider all options such as low-income housing programs and other non-traditional purchase methods.

Chapter **13**

NEGOTIATION

Whether you realize it or not, you are a negotiator. In fact, we all are. Any time two people make a joint decision, a negotiation takes place. If you convince a coworker to help you with a project at work, that is a negotiation. When your significant other agrees to give you a "massage" if you clean the kitchen, that is also a negotiation. These sort of situations arise every day and being an effective negotiator can become a powerful attribute in a person's professional and personal life.

The purpose of negotiating is to get what you want, right? Well, that may be the honest answer, but in order to be a successful negotiator, we need to expand on this definition. Instead, the purpose of negotiating is to reach an outcome that is mutually beneficial for all the parties involved. You want a situation in which everyone wins and walks away feeling good. If a mutually beneficial agreement is not reached, then it is not a negotiation, but simply one person taking advantage of the other.

Know your Opponent

The secret to achieving a mutually beneficial arrangement and the first step in the negotiation process is to place yourself in the other person's shoes. You need to figure out exactly what he is trying to achieve from the negotiation and how important each of those achievements is. Unless you know the other person's desires, it is hard to meet them and even harder to reach a mutually beneficial agreement.

> **Example 1:** Negotiating with your roommate. Let's say that you hate cleaning the bathroom and want to convince your roommate to do it instead. You cannot just tell her to do it—you need to negotiate. So put yourself in her shoes. Consider what she doesn't like to do. Maybe you know that your roommate hates doing the dishes so you offer to do the dishes if she will clean the bathroom. Everyone wins.

> **Example 2:** Buying a house. When most people purchase real estate, they simply write up an offer and hope the seller agrees. This obviously works, but instead of just crossing your fingers and hoping your offer is accepted, it is probably better to do a little negotiating with the seller. Price is not always the main concern

and by sitting down with the seller and having a brief discussion, his priorities may be revealed. Find out what the seller is going to do with the sale proceeds, how soon the deal needs to close, what other offers have been received, and any other relevant information. Having this knowledge will put you in a much better position to negotiate a good deal. It's not uncommon for sellers to choose a lower offer because they want to close the deal quickly or even because they simply like that buyer.

Be Nice

The best salesman and the best negotiator I have ever known is my good friend "Smiley." Really, that's what everyone calls him. He's the kind of guy who could sell ice to an Eskimo, but would never do so because Eskimos don't need ice and he would not want to take advantage. His name describes him perfectly. He is friendly, outgoing, and always smiling. Having such a personality allows him to be an outstanding negotiator. During a recent trip to Las Vegas, I witnessed Smiley at full force. With margarita in hand, Smiley negotiated free entrance to an elite club, free tickets to a comedy show at Ceaser's, and best of all, a complimentary lobster dinner after losing a whopping $30 at blackjack. He didn't really deserve any of this, but a little friendliness can go a long way.

Before you even begin to negotiate, have a friendly chat, get to know the other party, and allow them get to know you. This way you will be considered more of a friend than an adversary and are more likely to be helped out. If you go into a negotiation thinking you're going to bully the other party into giving you what you want, you will likely be disappointed with the results. This approach may have worked on the elementary school playground, but it won't fly in the real world.

He Who Speaks First Loses

Yeah, yeah, yeah. We have all heard this cliché. The problem is that everyone knows it and therefore avoids speaking first. You should at least attempt to get the other person to make the first offer by asking questions such as "How much were you thinking?" or "What would you like to do about this?" However, many people will not respond directly to these questions, resulting in a back-and-forth interrogation in which neither party budges. It can get ridiculous if it goes on for too long and you may want to chime in with an offer. It is okay to speak first as long as your first offer is far from what the other party is willing to accept. If you're buying a used car for example, offer a couple thousand below what you think the seller is willing to accept. Don't make your initial offer too ridiculous or else you may insult the other party, but definitely do lowball them.

Tit for Tat

In most negotiations, there is a back-and-forth dynamic until a final agreement is reached. During this process, there are many more things to negotiate besides price, or whatever is the main purpose for the negotiation. Any time that the other party asks for something, you should ask for something as well. Tit for tat – it's only fair. For example, let's say that you are buying a new wakeboard boat from a dealership. While bickering back and forth about price, you make your final offer of $28,000. The salesman holds his ground, refusing to go below $29,000. Assuming this price is agreeable to you, don't just say OK. Instead, say something like "OK, I'll do $29,000 if you throw in a free wakeboard." Other things you could throw into the mix are store credit, extended warranties, and upgrades on the boat. The salesman is often so focused on price that he may be happier to receive a higher price even if he has to give away store credit or a wakeboard. If you are going to give something away in a negotiation, you should receive something as well. Tit for tat.

Know Your Limit

Before entering into a negotiation, you should always know how far you are willing to go and at what point you will walk away from the table. It is important to set this limit before you enter the negotiation so that you can avoid making emotionally driven decisions in the heat of the moment. If you are trying to buy something, set a price limit for how much you are willing to pay and stick to it. It can be hard to walk away from a negotiation, but it can also be necessary. It is important to have the self-discipline to walk away if you cannot reach an acceptable agreement.

Negotiating As a Customer

The preceding discussion is relevant for most negotiations, but it does not necessarily apply to negotiating as a customer, when the squeaky wheel does get the oil and assertiveness is rewarded. People often underestimate their power as a consumer. We have all heard the saying "The customer is always right," but people rarely seem to exercise that power. Customers or clients are the lifeline of every business. Without them, the business would have no income and could not exist. Therefore, businesses strive to keep customers happy. Let me give an example to better explain my point.

We've all been hit with fees from a bank at one time or another, right? Well, next time you get a fee such as a minimum balance fee, try this: Call customer service and say, "Hi, I saw that I was charged a fee the other day, why was that?" The bank representative will give you some B.S. reason that was hidden amongst the small print and then you simply ask to have that fee credited back to your account. They may agree to do so or they may say "sorry, it's our policy to charge a fee when a customer's balance falls below the minimum." If it's the latter, ask to speak with the supervisor and explain the problem. Say something like "Hi, I realize that your bank's policy is to charge fees for low balances. That creates a problem for us, because I have a policy as well. My policy is that I don't pay those kinds of fees. Is there a way that we can still do business?" You will be surprised how many banks will give in to this sort of situation. Give it a try sometime.

This "Sorry, I too have a policy" strategy is of course not limited to bank account fees—it can work in a variety of situations. Just don't take things in life as given. Policies and rules were created as guidelines. They are not carved in stone or ordained by God. They are meant to be broken when appropriate. Standing by some nonsense policy is often not worth losing a good customer and businesses know this. So when a bank charges you a fee or a salesman says that he doesn't give quotes over the phone or when a realtor claims that you can only speak with a seller through her and not directly, tell them "That's too bad because I have this policy…" Don't be a jerk about it, but do be firm and hold your ground. You will likely get your way.

If You Don't Ask the Question, You Won't Get the Answer

You would be amazed at how much you can get in life if you just ask for it. Wherever you are, if you want something, simply ask for it. It's surprising how many salespeople, customer service representatives, and managers are willing to give in to your consumer requests. For example, a few weeks ago my brother accidentally flew a remote control helicopter over some fences and lost it. He called up the manufacturer and asked them if there was any way that he could get a new one. Sure enough, a week later there was a free helicopter on his doorstep. The manufacturer had absolutely no fault or responsibility for the helicopter being lost, but they sent my brother a new one anyway, simply because he asked. The key is to ask the question and then just wait for a response. If you give them a way out by saying something like "It's cool if you can't do that" or "If not, don't worry about it," they will jump on the prompt. Simply ask for what you want and then just wait for their response. Generally speaking, human beings tend to avoid conflict. It is much easier to just give customers what they want than argue with them. Give it a try sometime. You may be surprised at the results you can get by simply asking the question.

Chapter 13: What It's All About

Negotiation is the process of getting your way while simultaneously helping others. This invaluable skill has undeniable benefits whether you are purchasing a piece of real estate or just hanging out with friends.

CLOSING
THOUGHTS

This book is about money—how to make it and how to protect it. This is an extremely important topic as money makes the world go around and can provide us with the means to accomplish our dreams. Unfortunately, it is all too common for people to get confused about money's role in society. The purpose of money is an extremely individualistic concept. My reasons for accumulating wealth may vary drastically from yours. I'm not here to tell you whether your attitude regarding money is right or wrong, justified or ridiculous. But I would like to give you a little glimpse into my perspective. I believe that money is a tool and nothing more. Most people would consider money to be a tool for simply accumulating material goods. I have a broader view. Yes, money is great for obtaining material items, but that is only one of its many uses. To me, money is a ticket to freedom. I don't care for Escalades, giant TVs, or Armani suits—that's not why I want money. I want money because a wealthy individual does not need to concern him or herself with making ends meet. A wealthy individual does not need to work if he or she does not care to. A wealthy individual is financially free and has the means to pursue his or her true desires. I want money so that I can create unforgettable life experiences and become emotionally wealthy, not to accumulate material wealth. After all, in the end, all we have is memories. When you are lying on your deathbed, what will you reflect upon and value the most—the life you shared with your friends and family or your Mercedes? The point is simple: A Mercedes costs $40,000, but memories are priceless. When I'm 85 years old, I want to tell my grandchildren stories about my crazy times in college and how I won the heart of their grandmother and about a surfing trip to Costa Rica—not about the granite countertops and leather couch I used to own. Money is a tool for accomplishing your desires, whatever they may be. It is nothing more than a tool, so do not fall in love with the idea of simply having money. The most successful person in the room is not the one with the biggest wallet, but the one with the biggest smile. This life is not a dress rehearsal—it's the only shot you get. So be smart with your money, enjoy yourself, and live life to the fullest.